Mometrix

TEST PREPARATION

Secrets of the

ACSM®

Registered Clinical Exercise Physiologist Exam Study Guide

DEAR FUTURE EXAM SUCCESS STORY

First of all, **THANK YOU** for purchasing Mometrix study materials!

Second, congratulations! You are one of the few determined test-takers who are committed to doing whatever it takes to excel on your exam. **You have come to the right place.** We developed these study materials with one goal in mind: to deliver you the information you need in a format that's concise and easy to use.

In addition to optimizing your guide for the content of the test, we've outlined our recommended steps for breaking down the preparation process into small, attainable goals so you can make sure you stay on track.

We've also analyzed the entire test-taking process, identifying the most common pitfalls and showing how you can overcome them and be ready for any curveball the test throws you.

Standardized testing is one of the biggest obstacles on your road to success, which only increases the importance of doing well in the high-pressure, high-stakes environment of test day. Your results on this test could have a significant impact on your future, and this guide provides the information and practical advice to help you achieve your full potential on test day.

Your success is our success

We would love to hear from you! If you would like to share the story of your exam success or if you have any questions or comments in regard to our products, please contact us at **800-673-8175** or **support@mometrix.com**.

Thanks again for your business and we wish you continued success!

Sincerely,
The Mometrix Test Preparation Team

Need more help? Check out our flashcards at:
http://MometrixFlashcards.com/ACSM

Written and edited by the Mometrix Exam Secrets Test Prep Team
Printed in the United States of America

TABLE OF CONTENTS

Introduction

Thank you for purchasing this resource! You have made the choice to prepare yourself for a test that could have a huge impact on your future, and this guide is designed to help you be fully ready for test day. Obviously, it's important to have a solid understanding of the test material, but you also need to be prepared for the unique environment and stressors of the test, so that you can perform to the best of your abilities.

For this purpose, the first section that appears in this guide is the **Secret Keys**. We've devoted countless hours to meticulously researching what works and what doesn't, and we've boiled down our findings to the five most impactful steps you can take to improve your performance on the test. We start at the beginning with study planning and move through the preparation process, all the way to the testing strategies that will help you get the most out of what you know when you're finally sitting in front of the test.

We recommend that you start preparing for your test as far in advance as possible. However, if you've bought this guide as a last-minute study resource and only have a few days before your test, we recommend that you skip over the first two Secret Keys since they address a long-term study plan.

If you struggle with **test anxiety**, we strongly encourage you to check out our recommendations for how you can overcome it. Test anxiety is a formidable foe, but it can be beaten, and we want to make sure you have the tools you need to defeat it.

Secret Key 1: Plan Big, Study Small

There's a lot riding on your performance. If you want to ace this test, you're going to need to keep your skills sharp and the material fresh in your mind. You need a plan that lets you review everything you need to know while still fitting in your schedule. We'll break this strategy down into three categories.

Information Organization

Start with the information you already have: the official test outline. From this, you can make a complete list of all the concepts you need to cover before the test. Organize these concepts into groups that can be studied together, and create a list of any related vocabulary you need to learn so you can brush up on any difficult terms. You'll want to keep this vocabulary list handy once you actually start studying since you may need to add to it along the way.

Time Management

Once you have your set of study concepts, decide how to spread them out over the time you have left before the test. Break your study plan into small, clear goals so you have a manageable task for each day and know exactly what you're doing. Then just focus on one small step at a time. When you manage your time this way, you don't need to spend hours at a time studying. Studying a small block of content for a short period each day helps you retain information better and avoid stressing over how much you have left to do. You can relax knowing that you have a plan to cover everything in time. In order for this strategy to be effective though, you have to start studying early and stick to your schedule. Avoid the exhaustion and futility that comes from last-minute cramming!

Study Environment

The environment you study in has a big impact on your learning. Studying in a coffee shop, while probably more enjoyable, is not likely to be as fruitful as studying in a quiet room. It's important to keep distractions to a minimum. You're only planning to study for a short block of time, so make the most of it. Don't pause to check your phone or get up to find a snack. It's also important to **avoid multitasking**. Research has consistently shown that multitasking will make your studying dramatically less effective. Your study area should also be comfortable and well-lit so you don't have the distraction of straining your eyes or sitting on an uncomfortable chair.

The time of day you study is also important. You want to be rested and alert. Don't wait until just before bedtime. Study when you'll be most likely to comprehend and remember. Even better, if you know what time of day your test will be, set that time aside for study. That way your brain will be used to working on that subject at that specific time and you'll have a better chance of recalling information.

Finally, it can be helpful to team up with others who are studying for the same test. Your actual studying should be done in as isolated an environment as possible, but the work of organizing the information and setting up the study plan can be divided up. In between study sessions, you can discuss with your teammates the concepts that you're all studying and quiz each other on the details. Just be sure that your teammates are as serious about the test as you are. If you find that your study time is being replaced with social time, you might need to find a new team.

Secret Key 2: Make Your Studying Count

You're devoting a lot of time and effort to preparing for this test, so you want to be absolutely certain it will pay off. This means doing more than just reading the content and hoping you can remember it on test day. It's important to make every minute of study count. There are two main areas you can focus on to make your studying count.

Retention

It doesn't matter how much time you study if you can't remember the material. You need to make sure you are retaining the concepts. To check your retention of the information you're learning, try recalling it at later times with minimal prompting. Try carrying around flashcards and glance at one or two from time to time or ask a friend who's also studying for the test to quiz you.

To enhance your retention, look for ways to put the information into practice so that you can apply it rather than simply recalling it. If you're using the information in practical ways, it will be much easier to remember. Similarly, it helps to solidify a concept in your mind if you're not only reading it to yourself but also explaining it to someone else. Ask a friend to let you teach them about a concept you're a little shaky on (or speak aloud to an imaginary audience if necessary). As you try to summarize, define, give examples, and answer your friend's questions, you'll understand the concepts better and they will stay with you longer. Finally, step back for a big picture view and ask yourself how each piece of information fits with the whole subject. When you link the different concepts together and see them working together as a whole, it's easier to remember the individual components.

Finally, practice showing your work on any multi-step problems, even if you're just studying. Writing out each step you take to solve a problem will help solidify the process in your mind, and you'll be more likely to remember it during the test.

Modality

Modality simply refers to the means or method by which you study. Choosing a study modality that fits your own individual learning style is crucial. No two people learn best in exactly the same way, so it's important to know your strengths and use them to your advantage.

For example, if you learn best by visualization, focus on visualizing a concept in your mind and draw an image or a diagram. Try color-coding your notes, illustrating them, or creating symbols that will trigger your mind to recall a learned concept. If you learn best by hearing or discussing information, find a study partner who learns the same way or read aloud to yourself. Think about how to put the information in your own words. Imagine that you are giving a lecture on the topic and record yourself so you can listen to it later.

For any learning style, flashcards can be helpful. Organize the information so you can take advantage of spare moments to review. Underline key words or phrases. Use different colors for different categories. Mnemonic devices (such as creating a short list in which every item starts with the same letter) can also help with retention. Find what works best for you and use it to store the information in your mind most effectively and easily.

Secret Key 3: Practice the Right Way

Your success on test day depends not only on how many hours you put into preparing, but also on whether you prepared the right way. It's good to check along the way to see if your studying is paying off. One of the most effective ways to do this is by taking practice tests to evaluate your progress. Practice tests are useful because they show exactly where you need to improve. Every time you take a practice test, pay special attention to these three groups of questions:

- The questions you got wrong
- The questions you had to guess on, even if you guessed right
- The questions you found difficult or slow to work through

This will show you exactly what your weak areas are, and where you need to devote more study time. Ask yourself why each of these questions gave you trouble. Was it because you didn't understand the material? Was it because you didn't remember the vocabulary? Do you need more repetitions on this type of question to build speed and confidence? Dig into those questions and figure out how you can strengthen your weak areas as you go back to review the material.

Additionally, many practice tests have a section explaining the answer choices. It can be tempting to read the explanation and think that you now have a good understanding of the concept. However, an explanation likely only covers part of the question's broader context. Even if the explanation makes perfect sense, **go back and investigate** every concept related to the question until you're positive you have a thorough understanding.

As you go along, keep in mind that the practice test is just that: practice. Memorizing these questions and answers will not be very helpful on the actual test because it is unlikely to have any of the same exact questions. If you only know the right answers to the sample questions, you won't be prepared for the real thing. **Study the concepts** until you understand them fully, and then you'll be able to answer any question that shows up on the test.

It's important to wait on the practice tests until you're ready. If you take a test on your first day of study, you may be overwhelmed by the amount of material covered and how much you need to learn. Work up to it gradually.

On test day, you'll need to be prepared for answering questions, managing your time, and using the test-taking strategies you've learned. It's a lot to balance, like a mental marathon that will have a big impact on your future. Like training for a marathon, you'll need to start slowly and work your way up. When test day arrives, you'll be ready.

Start with the strategies you've read in the first two Secret Keys—plan your course and study in the way that works best for you. If you have time, consider using multiple study resources to get different approaches to the same concepts. It can be helpful to see difficult concepts from more than one angle. Then find a good source for practice tests. Many times, the test website will suggest potential study resources or provide sample tests.

Practice Test Strategy

If you're able to find at least three practice tests, we recommend this strategy:

Untimed and Open-Book Practice

Take the first test with no time constraints and with your notes and study guide handy. Take your time and focus on applying the strategies you've learned.

Timed and Open-Book Practice

Take the second practice test open-book as well, but set a timer and practice pacing yourself to finish in time.

Timed and Closed-Book Practice

Take any other practice tests as if it were test day. Set a timer and put away your study materials. Sit at a table or desk in a quiet room, imagine yourself at the testing center, and answer questions as quickly and accurately as possible.

Keep repeating timed and closed-book tests on a regular basis until you run out of practice tests or it's time for the actual test. Your mind will be ready for the schedule and stress of test day, and you'll be able to focus on recalling the material you've learned.

Secret Key 4: Pace Yourself

Once you're fully prepared for the material on the test, your biggest challenge on test day will be managing your time. Just knowing that the clock is ticking can make you panic even if you have plenty of time left. Work on pacing yourself so you can build confidence against the time constraints of the exam. Pacing is a difficult skill to master, especially in a high-pressure environment, so **practice is vital**.

Set time expectations for your pace based on how much time is available. For example, if a section has 60 questions and the time limit is 30 minutes, you know you have to average 30 seconds or less per question in order to answer them all. Although 30 seconds is the hard limit, set 25 seconds per question as your goal, so you reserve extra time to spend on harder questions. When you budget extra time for the harder questions, you no longer have any reason to stress when those questions take longer to answer.

Don't let this time expectation distract you from working through the test at a calm, steady pace, but keep it in mind so you don't spend too much time on any one question. Recognize that taking extra time on one question you don't understand may keep you from answering two that you do understand later in the test. If your time limit for a question is up and you're still not sure of the answer, mark it and move on, and come back to it later if the time and the test format allow. If the testing format doesn't allow you to return to earlier questions, just make an educated guess; then put it out of your mind and move on.

On the easier questions, be careful not to rush. It may seem wise to hurry through them so you have more time for the challenging ones, but it's not worth missing one if you know the concept and just didn't take the time to read the question fully. Work efficiently but make sure you understand the question and have looked at all of the answer choices, since more than one may seem right at first.

Even if you're paying attention to the time, you may find yourself a little behind at some point. You should speed up to get back on track, but do so wisely. Don't panic; just take a few seconds less on each question until you're caught up. Don't guess without thinking, but do look through the answer choices and eliminate any you know are wrong. If you can get down to two choices, it is often worthwhile to guess from those. Once you've chosen an answer, move on and don't dwell on any that you skipped or had to hurry through. If a question was taking too long, chances are it was one of the harder ones, so you weren't as likely to get it right anyway.

On the other hand, if you find yourself getting ahead of schedule, it may be beneficial to slow down a little. The more quickly you work, the more likely you are to make a careless mistake that will affect your score. You've budgeted time for each question, so don't be afraid to spend that time. Practice an efficient but careful pace to get the most out of the time you have.

Secret Key 5: Have a Plan for Guessing

When you're taking the test, you may find yourself stuck on a question. Some of the answer choices seem better than others, but you don't see the one answer choice that is obviously correct. What do you do?

The scenario described above is very common, yet most test takers have not effectively prepared for it. Developing and practicing a plan for guessing may be one of the single most effective uses of your time as you get ready for the exam.

In developing your plan for guessing, there are three questions to address:

- When should you start the guessing process?
- How should you narrow down the choices?
- Which answer should you choose?

When to Start the Guessing Process

Unless your plan for guessing is to select C every time (which, despite its merits, is not what we recommend), you need to leave yourself enough time to apply your answer elimination strategies. Since you have a limited amount of time for each question, that means that if you're going to give yourself the best shot at guessing correctly, you have to decide quickly whether or not you will guess.

Of course, the best-case scenario is that you don't have to guess at all, so first, see if you can answer the question based on your knowledge of the subject and basic reasoning skills. Focus on the key words in the question and try to jog your memory of related topics. Give yourself a chance to bring the knowledge to mind, but once you realize that you don't have (or you can't access) the knowledge you need to answer the question, it's time to start the guessing process.

It's almost always better to start the guessing process too early than too late. It only takes a few seconds to remember something and answer the question from knowledge. Carefully eliminating wrong answer choices takes longer. Plus, going through the process of eliminating answer choices can actually help jog your memory.

Summary: Start the guessing process as soon as you decide that you can't answer the question based on your knowledge.

How to Narrow Down the Choices

The next chapter in this book (**Test-Taking Strategies**) includes a wide range of strategies for how to approach questions and how to look for answer choices to eliminate. You will definitely want to read those carefully, practice them, and figure out which ones work best for you. Here though, we're going to address a mindset rather than a particular strategy.

Your odds of guessing an answer correctly depend on how many options you are choosing from.

Number of options left	5	4	3	2	1
Odds of guessing correctly	20%	25%	33%	50%	100%

You can see from this chart just how valuable it is to be able to eliminate incorrect answers and make an educated guess, but there are two things that many test takers do that cause them to miss out on the benefits of guessing:

- Accidentally eliminating the correct answer
- Selecting an answer based on an impression

We'll look at the first one here, and the second one in the next section.

To avoid accidentally eliminating the correct answer, we recommend a thought exercise called **the $5 challenge**. In this challenge, you only eliminate an answer choice from contention if you are willing to bet $5 on it being wrong. Why $5? Five dollars is a small but not insignificant amount of money. It's an amount you could afford to lose but wouldn't want to throw away. And while losing $5 once might not hurt too much, doing it twenty times will set you back $100. In the same way, each small decision you make—eliminating a choice here, guessing on a question there—won't by itself impact your score very much, but when you put them all together, they can make a big difference. By holding each answer choice elimination decision to a higher standard, you can reduce the risk of accidentally eliminating the correct answer.

The $5 challenge can also be applied in a positive sense: If you are willing to bet $5 that an answer choice *is* correct, go ahead and mark it as correct.

Summary: Only eliminate an answer choice if you are willing to bet $5 that it is wrong.

Which Answer to Choose

You're taking the test. You've run into a hard question and decided you'll have to guess. You've eliminated all the answer choices you're willing to bet $5 on. Now you have to pick an answer. Why do we even need to talk about this? Why can't you just pick whichever one you feel like when the time comes?

The answer to these questions is that if you don't come into the test with a plan, you'll rely on your impression to select an answer choice, and if you do that, you risk falling into a trap. The test writers know that everyone who takes their test will be guessing on some of the questions, so they intentionally write wrong answer choices to seem plausible. You still have to pick an answer though, and if the wrong answer choices are designed to look right, how can you ever be sure that you're not falling for their trap? The best solution we've found to this dilemma is to take the decision out of your hands entirely. Here is the process we recommend:

Once you've eliminated any choices that you are confident (willing to bet $5) are wrong, select the first remaining choice as your answer.

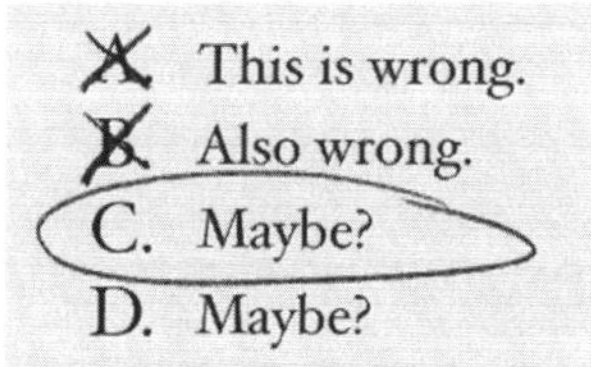

Whether you choose to select the first remaining choice, the second, or the last, the important thing is that you use some preselected standard. Using this approach guarantees that you will not be enticed into selecting an answer choice that looks right, because you are not basing your decision on how the answer choices look.

This is not meant to make you question your knowledge. Instead, it is to help you recognize the difference between your knowledge and your impressions. There's a huge difference between thinking an answer is right because of what you know, and thinking an answer is right because it looks or sounds like it should be right.

Summary: To ensure that your selection is appropriately random, make a predetermined selection from among all answer choices you have not eliminated.

Test-Taking Strategies

This section contains a list of test-taking strategies that you may find helpful as you work through the test. By taking what you know and applying logical thought, you can maximize your chances of answering any question correctly!

It is very important to realize that every question is different and every person is different: no single strategy will work on every question, and no single strategy will work for every person. That's why we've included all of them here, so you can try them out and determine which ones work best for different types of questions and which ones work best for you.

Question Strategies

✓ Read Carefully

Read the question and the answer choices carefully. Don't miss the question because you misread the terms. You have plenty of time to read each question thoroughly and make sure you understand what is being asked. Yet a happy medium must be attained, so don't waste too much time. You must read carefully and efficiently.

✓ Contextual Clues

Look for contextual clues. If the question includes a word you are not familiar with, look at the immediate context for some indication of what the word might mean. Contextual clues can often give you all the information you need to decipher the meaning of an unfamiliar word. Even if you can't determine the meaning, you may be able to narrow down the possibilities enough to make a solid guess at the answer to the question.

✓ Prefixes

If you're having trouble with a word in the question or answer choices, try dissecting it. Take advantage of every clue that the word might include. Prefixes can be a huge help. Usually, they allow you to determine a basic meaning. *Pre-* means before, *post-* means after, *pro-* is positive, *de-* is negative. From prefixes, you can get an idea of the general meaning of the word and try to put it into context.

✓ Hedge Words

Watch out for critical hedge words, such as *likely, may, can, often, almost, mostly, usually, generally, rarely,* and *sometimes.* Question writers insert these hedge phrases to cover every possibility. Often an answer choice will be wrong simply because it leaves no room for exception. Be on guard for answer choices that have definitive words such as *exactly* and *always.*

☑ SWITCHBACK WORDS

Stay alert for *switchbacks*. These are the words and phrases frequently used to alert you to shifts in thought. The most common switchback words are *but*, *although*, and *however*. Others include *nevertheless*, *on the other hand*, *even though*, *while*, *in spite of*, *despite*, and *regardless of*. Switchback words are important to catch because they can change the direction of the question or an answer choice.

☑ FACE VALUE

When in doubt, use common sense. Accept the situation in the problem at face value. Don't read too much into it. These problems will not require you to make wild assumptions. If you have to go beyond creativity and warp time or space in order to have an answer choice fit the question, then you should move on and consider the other answer choices. These are normal problems rooted in reality. The applicable relationship or explanation may not be readily apparent, but it is there for you to figure out. Use your common sense to interpret anything that isn't clear.

Answer Choice Strategies

☑ ANSWER SELECTION

The most thorough way to pick an answer choice is to identify and eliminate wrong answers until only one is left, then confirm it is the correct answer. Sometimes an answer choice may immediately seem right, but be careful. The test writers will usually put more than one reasonable answer choice on each question, so take a second to read all of them and make sure that the other choices are not equally obvious. As long as you have time left, it is better to read every answer choice than to pick the first one that looks right without checking the others.

☑ ANSWER CHOICE FAMILIES

An answer choice family consists of two (in rare cases, three) answer choices that are very similar in construction and cannot all be true at the same time. If you see two answer choices that are direct opposites or parallels, one of them is usually the correct answer. For instance, if one answer choice says that quantity x increases and another either says that quantity x decreases (opposite) or says that quantity y increases (parallel), then those answer choices would fall into the same family. An answer choice that doesn't match the construction of the answer choice family is more likely to be incorrect. Most questions will not have answer choice families, but when they do appear, you should be prepared to recognize them.

☑ ELIMINATE ANSWERS

Eliminate answer choices as soon as you realize they are wrong, but make sure you consider all possibilities. If you are eliminating answer choices and realize that the last one you are left with is also wrong, don't panic. Start over and consider each choice again. There may be something you missed the first time that you will realize on the second pass.

✓ Avoid Fact Traps

Don't be distracted by an answer choice that is factually true but doesn't answer the question. You are looking for the choice that answers the question. Stay focused on what the question is asking for so you don't accidentally pick an answer that is true but incorrect. Always go back to the question and make sure the answer choice you've selected actually answers the question and is not merely a true statement.

✓ Extreme Statements

In general, you should avoid answers that put forth extreme actions as standard practice or proclaim controversial ideas as established fact. An answer choice that states the "process should be used in certain situations, if..." is much more likely to be correct than one that states the "process should be discontinued completely." The first is a calm rational statement and doesn't even make a definitive, uncompromising stance, using a hedge word *if* to provide wiggle room, whereas the second choice is far more extreme.

✓ Benchmark

As you read through the answer choices and you come across one that seems to answer the question well, mentally select that answer choice. This is not your final answer, but it's the one that will help you evaluate the other answer choices. The one that you selected is your benchmark or standard for judging each of the other answer choices. Every other answer choice must be compared to your benchmark. That choice is correct until proven otherwise by another answer choice beating it. If you find a better answer, then that one becomes your new benchmark. Once you've decided that no other choice answers the question as well as your benchmark, you have your final answer.

✓ Predict the Answer

Before you even start looking at the answer choices, it is often best to try to predict the answer. When you come up with the answer on your own, it is easier to avoid distractions and traps because you will know exactly what to look for. The right answer choice is unlikely to be word-for-word what you came up with, but it should be a close match. Even if you are confident that you have the right answer, you should still take the time to read each option before moving on.

General Strategies

✓ Tough Questions

If you are stumped on a problem or it appears too hard or too difficult, don't waste time. Move on! Remember though, if you can quickly check for obviously incorrect answer choices, your chances of guessing correctly are greatly improved. Before you completely give up, at least try to knock out a couple of possible answers. Eliminate what you can and then guess at the remaining answer choices before moving on.

✓ Check Your Work

Since you will probably not know every term listed and the answer to every question, it is important that you get credit for the ones that you do know. Don't miss any questions through careless mistakes. If at all possible, try to take a second to look back over your answer selection and make sure you've selected the correct answer choice and haven't made a costly careless mistake (such as marking an answer choice that you didn't mean to mark). This quick double check should more than pay for itself in caught mistakes for the time it costs.

✓ Pace Yourself

It's easy to be overwhelmed when you're looking at a page full of questions; your mind is confused and full of random thoughts, and the clock is ticking down faster than you would like. Calm down and maintain the pace that you have set for yourself. Especially as you get down to the last few minutes of the test, don't let the small numbers on the clock make you panic. As long as you are on track by monitoring your pace, you are guaranteed to have time for each question.

✓ Don't Rush

It is very easy to make errors when you are in a hurry. Maintaining a fast pace in answering questions is pointless if it makes you miss questions that you would have gotten right otherwise. Test writers like to include distracting information and wrong answers that seem right. Taking a little extra time to avoid careless mistakes can make all the difference in your test score. Find a pace that allows you to be confident in the answers that you select.

✓ Keep Moving

Panicking will not help you pass the test, so do your best to stay calm and keep moving. Taking deep breaths and going through the answer elimination steps you practiced can help to break through a stress barrier and keep your pace.

Final Notes

The combination of a solid foundation of content knowledge and the confidence that comes from practicing your plan for applying that knowledge is the key to maximizing your performance on test day. As your foundation of content knowledge is built up and strengthened, you'll find that the strategies included in this chapter become more and more effective in helping you quickly sift through the distractions and traps of the test to isolate the correct answer.

Now that you're preparing to move forward into the test content chapters of this book, be sure to keep your goal in mind. As you read, think about how you will be able to apply this information on the test. If you've already seen sample questions for the test and you have an idea of the question format and style, try to come up with questions of your own that you can answer based on what you're reading. This will give you valuable practice applying your knowledge in the same ways you can expect to on test day.

Good luck and good studying!

Clinical Assessment

Pre-Screening Process

During the pre-screening process, the exercise physiologist follows a series of steps to ensure the comfort of the patient and to ensure that nothing important is missed. The first step is to ask for the patient's express consent for the pre-screening. After receiving the patient's consent, the exercise physiologist takes a formal medical history for the patient. Often this step will reveal a number of potential risk factors or important points for the exercise physiologist to consider. The third step is to discuss exercise goals with the patient. This step is crucial for a successful program. Next, the exercise physiologist identifies the patient's risk factors. If an exercise test is appropriate, the exercise physiologist will recommend the test best suited to the patient's needs. The exercise physiologist has to decide if his or her facility can handle the testing or if the patient should be referred to another facility. The results of the exercise test help the specialist determine the best exercise program for the patient's health needs and fitness goals.

Medical Background

The fundamental goal of the exercise physiologist during pre-screening is to determine if a patient can safely begin an exercise program. During the course of pre-screening, the exercise physiologist may need to determine whether or not exercise testing is needed. The exercise physiologist will also recommend whether or not the patient needs medical supervision when beginning an exercise program, and if so, what degree of supervision is prudent. In the process of pre-screening, the exercise physiologist will identify what contraindications the patient has, if there are factors that put the patient at increased risk, and if the patient has any special needs. All this information will be used to design an exercise program appropriate for the patient.

During the medical history, the exercise physiologist needs to determine past or current events or conditions that may affect the patient's ability to exercise safely. Some of the things the exercise physiologist should ask about include diagnoses of chronic diseases or diseases with lasting effects, any hospitalizations or surgeries the patient has experienced, any medications that the patient is taking, and any family history of illness. The exercise physiologist should also ask about current activities that the patient engages in. It may be that the patient has recently undergone exercise testing. If so, the results of the test will be relevant to the evaluation. The specialist should also determine any existing symptoms that the patient is contending with and how frequent and severe the symptoms are.

Risk Factors

Risk factors, otherwise known as positive risk factors, are circumstances that increase the patient's risk of a condition or disease. A negative risk factor is one that provides protection against a condition or disease, lowering the patient's risk. Some of the risk factors the exercise physiologist should account for during the pre-screening process are the following: family history of disease; history of smoking or current smoking habit; high blood pressure; high cholesterol levels; high fasting glucose levels; obesity; and sedentary lifestyle. Negative risk factors include high levels of HDL cholesterol, an active lifestyle, and healthy eating habits.

Symptoms

The exercise physiologist is primarily concerned with symptoms that occur when the patient exerts himself or attempts to exercise. The most common symptoms that the exercise physiologist should take note of are pain or discomfort in the area of the chest; shortness of breath; high levels of fatigue triggered by physical activity; dizziness; heart palpitations or a confirmed heart murmur; pain in the legs; and breathing irregularities. Each of these symptoms can help to indicate to the specialist what problems the patient may encounter when exercising and how to develop a safe exercise program that will assist the patient in improving his or her condition.

Physical Factors

During the pre-screening process, the exercise physiologist screens physical factors as well as taking a medical history. As an exercise physiologist, you need to take a patient's blood pressure both when she is lying down on her back and when she is standing up. You also want to measure the patient's heart rate and blood pressure after mild exertion such as walking to the end of the hall and back. You should listen to the patient's heartbeat, checking for any abnormalities not listed in the patient's history. You should listen to the patient's lungs, as well. You will also take the patient's pulse and examine her musculoskeletal system for any abnormalities.

Lab Tests

There are several lab tests that an exercise physiologist might perform during a medical pre-screening. Among these are a complete blood count (CBC), a urinary analysis, a measure of blood glucose, a measure of creatine levels, and a measure of cholesterol levels. Each of these tests can indicate medical conditions that might determine the type of exercise program appropriate for the patient. For example, a CBC might uncover that the patient has anemia—low iron levels in the blood. Anemia can cause the patient to fatigue quickly, which would make strenuous exercise difficult. In this case you would need to address the anemia as well as tailor exercise recommendations appropriately. In some cases, EKG testing and other stress level testing also may be appropriate.

Contraindications

In some cases, exercise testing may present a danger to the patient. The exercise physiologist must recognize the contraindications that absolutely rule out exercise testing. Those contraindications include a recent heart attack or myocardial infarction, unstable angina, an uncontrolled arrhythmia, aortic stenosis with severe symptoms, uncontrolled heart failure, pulmonary embolus, the presence of a dissecting aneurysm, or the existence of an acute infection. In addition, some conditions require caution when testing, but testing may still be beneficial. (In these cases, the exercise physiologist or supervising physician must determine if the risks outweigh the benefits.) These include moderate arrhythmias, moderate cardiopulmonary conditions, metabolic disorders, bone disorders, or chronic infections. The exercise physiologist should also look for electrolyte imbalances, hypertension, or conditions that impair mobility.

Physical Examination

A place to start a pre-exercise physical examination is measurement of body weight and/or some other similar data point such as the body mass index (BMI). Most of the other important measurements are related to evidence of cardiovascular, pulmonary, or neuromuscular problems. In particular, blood pressure measurements should be performed in various positions while at rest. Both the heart and lungs should be listened to with the stethoscope for various sounds such as heart murmurs in the former and wheezing or crackling sounds in the latter. Pressure should be applied to various arteries to check for pulses and in some cases edema. The skin and tendons should be checked for evidence of lipid disorders. Orthopedic problems should be noted. Neurological evaluations should be performed. Diabetic individuals should have their skin checked as well.

Confidence Interval, Dose-Response Relationship, Epidemiology

Confidence interval: When gathering statistical evidence regarding the relative risks of different factors, researchers establish a confidence interval. This is a range of relative risk levels to increase certainty that the actual relative risk is addressed.

Dose-response relationship: In research, this refers to the effects on a factor caused by a change in another factor. If one variable is changed and causes a measurable change in another variable, the two have a dose-response relationship. The relationship may be inverse, direct, linear, curvilinear, quadratic, etc.

Epidemiology: This is the field of research that focuses on the incidence, prevalence, and causes of diseases and injuries

Exercise Capacity

Exercise capacity is a measure of the peak physical output someone can maintain for a period of time. In order to be deemed stable, an individual must be able to exert him or herself for an extended period of time.

Regular exercise and overall exercise capacity are important in part because of the impact they have on cardiovascular disease. Long-term studies demonstrate that physical fitness and exercise capacity have an inverse relationship to death caused by heart disease. Better fitness levels and a higher exercise capacity predict a higher survival rate in the face of heart disease and also protect against the development of heart disease.

Because physical fitness and exercise capacity increase survival rates, it is important that patients with cardiovascular diseases take steps to improve their health in these areas. Doing so can improve their overall outcome.

During the pre-screening interview, the exercise physiologist should ask the patient about physical activity that he has done recently and how it made him feel. This information will help to guide the exercise physiologist in fully understanding the patient's current habits and general exercise capacity. It can also make it easier to test exercise capacity in the laboratory.

During the interview, encourage the patient to be as detailed as possible. He should describe the type of activities he has done, how much work he did, for how long, and at what intensity. You should ask questions about the patient's physical state during the activity. Did he have to stop frequently to catch his breath? Was there pain or dizziness? Also, ask about conditions that might affect response like temperature and recent meals.

If the patient does not have any recent exercise experiences to describe, the exercise physiologist can ask about day-to-day activities like climbing the stairs or walking across a parking lot.

Inconsistent Exercise Capacity

Sometimes a patient will provide examples in the interview process that do not demonstrate a consistent exercise capacity. Generally, the exercise physiologist strives to determine a patient's exercise capacity as accurately as possible, but this can be difficult when there are inconsistencies that you must address.

Some inconsistencies can be accounted for based on the different types of exercise. Perhaps a patient can consistently climb stairs without issue, but demonstrates less capacity when activities involve arm strength. This is normal. Some patients may have a condition like fibromyalgia that varies from day to day, and their capacity may vary greatly between those days. In these cases, a range of exercise capacity may be most appropriate and also the best you can do.

Exercise-Related Symptoms

In the course of interviewing the patient, the exercise physiologist should pay particular attention to symptoms that the patient mentions arising during physical activity. Take particular note of symptoms that caused the patient to stop the activity. These symptoms will help you determine the range of exercise that the patient is capable of achieving and what limits she has.

The symptoms that typically put a stop to activity include chest pains, light-headedness, weakness or cramping. Determine the duration and intensity of exercise that resulted in the described symptoms. Also note how much resting time the patient required for recovery.

Measured in a Laboratory Setting

While a patient interview and history give the exercise physiologist a great deal of information about exercise capacity, an actual laboratory test measuring exercise capacity can provide objective information to more fully describe a patient's capacity.

In the lab, a patient will be monitored while they exercise (often on a treadmill). The goal is to bring the patient to her peak output and have her sustain it for a set period of time. During that time, total work output and oxygen consumption are measured. These numbers will show her current exercise capacity and also indicate if it is well below normal (an indication of deeper health problems). Also, the attending physician will track heart rate, blood pressure, and blood gas content.

Conditions

A limited exercise capacity is often the result of a specific condition. Measuring exercise capacity can be especially useful for diagnosing conditions that don't present symptoms when a person is not under exertion—this is why an exercise assessment is important even in healthy individuals who do not have an established exercise routine.

A limited exercise capacity can indicate aortic valve disease, a condition that puts the patient at a very high risk of death. In people with known cardiovascular disease, a limited exercise capacity also indicates a high risk of death. It is important to note that measuring exercise capacity will not catch all patients at risk of death from cardiac diseases.

Body Mass Index (BMI)

Body mass index or BMI is calculated as follows:

BMI = weight (kg)/height squared (m^2), usually represented as $kg \cdot m^{-2}$

From the BMI calculation, tables have been developed to predict percentage of body fat based on sex and age. In general, individuals with a BMI over 30 $kg \cdot m^{-2}$ are considered to be obese, while a value in the 25.0 to 29.9 $kg \cdot m^{-2}$ range is considered overweight, and values below that are generally termed normal. Associations between obese BMI levels and elevated risk of CAD, hypertension, low relative HDL cholesterol, and death have been found. In addition, individuals with very low BMI, less than 18.5 kg per square meter, have also been found to be more prone to cardiac problems.

Taking Measurements

Prior to the actual exercise testing, heart rate, blood pressure and ECG readings should be taken lying down as well as in the position in which the test will be performed. The BP and ECG measurements are actually done in a continuous manner. Good preparation of the lead interface skin portions is crucial to reduce noise in the ECG reading; only 3 leads instead of the full 12 leads are often checked or employed because of the movement. During and after the test, continuous electrocardiographic and heart rate monitoring should be performed and recorded toward the end of each stage or minute respectively. This monitoring should be continued after the actual test is terminated. Blood pressure measurements are typically taken toward the end of each cycle or the end of each 2 minute time period if ramp protocols are used, again right after the exercise, and then at 2 minute intervals.

Minimal Required Measurements

Two important tests should be taken at baseline before beginning exercise testing and during it as well, heart rate and blood pressure. A baseline ECG at rest might be done in addition. Further, there is usually a subjective measurement that the subject monitors himself called rating of perceived exertion, or RPE. There are various methods of obtaining the heart rate, generally by feeling it with the first and second fingers over either the wrist radial artery or neck carotid artery, listening to it through the sternum with the stethoscope, or using a heart rate monitor. Blood pressure measurements can be taken with a cuff over the upper arm and use of either a mercury sphygmomanometer or a manometer to measure gas pressure. RPE scales have been generated to self-rate exercise intensity.

Classification Guidelines

An apparently healthy individual has no restrictions for activity/exercise participation beyond common sense, nor is it usually necessary to supervise their activity or do any monitoring, although those in Classes A-2 or -3 might want to undergo a medical examination or exercise test. For, low risk individuals (Class B) it is best to tailor a program to the individual and have medical supervision initially, followed by supervision by other trained personnel. Cardiac monitoring by ECG and blood pressure measurements are initially useful for up to about a dozen sessions. If a patient is at more risk (Class C), sessions should be overseen by medical personnel until it has been determined that the regimen is established, and until that time ECG and blood pressure measurements should be taken continuously during the session. Class D should not be participating at all.

Medical History

A moderate to high risk individual should have a medical history, physical examination and some laboratory work done before beginning an exercise program. The medical history should include many components, particularly medical diagnosis as well as prior physical examination results and a history of their symptoms. The medical diagnosis should cover cardiovascular diseases and surgeries related to them and members of their family, in particular for valve disease, use of any implantable device such as a pacemaker, and other possible evidence of cardiovascular problems such as angina, hypertension, strokes, and blood clots in the veins. Pulmonary diseases, diabetes, malignancies, bone problems, being extremely overweight, and even psychological disorders should be observed. The most important features of previous physical examinations or history would be anything related to evidence of cardiac or pulmonary problems or abnormal laboratory findings. In addition, anything new like a recent illness should be noted, as well as orthopedic issues, medications being taken, and evidence of allergies to any drugs. Anything relevant to their ability to perform exercise such as current levels of activity at work or at home should be noted.

Measuring Heart Rate

The heart rate or pulse can be measured at any artery, but the most common ones used are the carotid or radial arteries. This is because these two arteries are both very large and located near the surface layer of the skin. There are actually two carotid arteries, both located in the neck either in the front or on the side. The radial artery is located on the inside of the forearm and is usually best found near the wrist. The pulse is taken by applying pressure with two fingers. Any arterial site that can be felt by palpation can be utilized.

Atherosclerosis

Atherosclerosis is a condition in which the aorta or other arteries have become occluded and blood flow is obstructed. This process occurs over time and primarily is due to deposition of fatty materials on the cell walls. It usually begins with some type of injury to the innermost layer or endothelium of the wall of one of the coronary arteries, which supply blood to the heart, or another vessel. An inflammatory process begins in which white blood cells called monocytes stick to the endothelium and move into the layer below called the intima. Cholesterol, specifically LDL-C, is absorbed, resulting in these fatty deposits. These monocytes as well as other cells such as platelets also stick to the inner wall layers and release various growth factors. Ultimately, plaques containing inflammatory cells and other deposits form inside the artery. As the plaque gets bigger in size, eventually vasoconstriction occurs.

A number of risk factors have been associated with increased risk of developing atherosclerosis. Some are better studied than others. Lipid profile abnormalities, in particular high levels of LDL-C coupled with low levels of HDL-C, are strongly correlated with atherosclerosis. The presence of hypertension, being relatively inactive or severely overweight, and having a family member who experienced a coronary problem at an early age all predispose individuals to atherosclerosis. In addition, some other biomarkers have been studied for their relationship to coronary disease. The ones that appear to be associated include C-reactive protein (CRP), which is a general immunological marker for inflammation; fibrinogen, which is a biological substance promoting clotting; some additional lipoproteins; and perhaps the amino acid homocysteine, which may injure the endothelium. Until menopause, women do not develop this disease as frequently as men.

Symptoms of Heart Disease

By far, the most important symptom of heart disease is discomfort in the chest or other upper body areas. Angina, or chest pains indicating a lack of blood to the heart, is the hallmark of cardiac disease. Since it is often manifested as more of a tight or burning feeling than an acute pain, the healthcare provider must be explicit in their questioning as to location and type of discomfort, changes upon exertion, and the response to nitroglycerin use. Presence of very fast or irregular heartbeats or swelling in the extremities suggests heart disease as well. Some other indications of underlying cardiac problems appear to be related to the pulmonary system such as experiencing dyspnea under a variety of circumstances at rest or upon exertion or coughing.

PHYSICAL EXAMINATION FOR HEART DISEASE

Another medical professional, not the doctor, may initially check vital signs and anthropometric measurements during a physical examination. The physician usually then begins his physical examination by merely making observations as to the subject's outward manifestations of possible problems. For heart disease, the doctor looks at the skin to see if it is a blue or purple color indicating lack of oxygen to the blood, if there are any broken or infected areas, whether there is any swelling in the limbs, and if there is any evidence of what is called clubbing in the digits. They also check the jugular vein to see if it is swollen. The doctor then feels a number of different arterial sites by applying finger pressure or palpation; this is done to not only check for heart rates but also abnormal patterns and swelling. The physician then usually taps or percusses various organs although this procedure is more valuable for other types of diagnoses. Then the doctor listens to the lungs and heart with a stethoscope for signs of cardio or respiratory disease. An electrocardiogram while at rest and chest radiograph are often routinely performed as well.

After compiling information from the history, physical examination and diagnostic tests, a physician has to make a differential diagnosis, where he looks at the totality of information available to determine the underlying cause(s) of symptoms. For chest discomfort, angina is only one cardiac disease that could be the cause. Others include an actual heart attack, heart valve problems, inflammation of the pericardial sac, or constriction or severing of the aorta. Pulmonary problems might give similar discomfort such as a blood clot in the lungs or pneumonia. Upper torso issues involving either the gastrointestinal tract, such as esophageal reflux, or the muscles of the spine could present similarly. The physician always needs to consider the cardiac risk category a patient falls into.

CONGESTIVE HEART FAILURE

Congestive heart failure is a condition in which the heart cannot effectively pump oxygenated blood to be used by tissues. It is actually the progression of what is usually called chronic heart failure (CHF), which refers to the inability of the ventricle to properly accept or expel blood. The main reason this occurs is because of some sort of malfunction of the left ventricle, primarily during systole but alternatively during diastole for a smaller percentage of patients. Typically, this disease progresses to the point where there is fluid overload in the heart or congestion and enlargement of the heart. Patients usually exhibit shortness of breath upon exercise and may not tolerate exercise well.

CARDIOMYOPATHIES

Cardiomyopathies are any of a number of cardiac abnormalities in which the heart muscle itself has been weakened enough to disrupt normal pumping action. If all 4 compartments in the heart have become enlarged, a condition called dilated cardiomyopathy occurs in which the ability to fill up with blood during systole is impaired. If some section of either ventricle enlarges relative to other parts, hypertrophic cardiomyopathy can result. Occasionally, a restrictive form of cardiomyopathy is observed in which the main abnormality is impaired ventricular ability to fill up with blood and a depressed stroke volume. There is also an uncommon inherited malignant disease which causes abnormal rhythm patterns in the right ventricle.

Cardiac Valvular Diseases

If a valve is somehow damaged by an infection such as rheumatic fever or an inherited abnormality, one of two types of valvular disease can occur. In the first, valvular stenosis, the surge of blood through the valve is hindered because the flaps are not working properly or there is a narrowing of the opening. Stenosis is primarily found at the aortic or mitral valves and can be predicted by hearing a murmur with the stethoscope. The other type of valvular disease is valvular regurgitation in which the blood actually flows backwards because the valve does not close properly. This condition has been found at all four cardiac valves, but again occurs more commonly at the aortic and mitral valves. Murmurs or evidence of enlargement are hallmarks.

Congenital Heart Diseases

A congenital heart disease is one that was inherited and present when the individual was born. Most should be repaired during childhood but if they are not, several types of these diseases can be found in adults. The most common deficiencies involve holes in the membranes of one of the heart chambers. Several types of atrial septal defects depending on the location of the hole, and ventricular septal defects can occur as well. Other types of defects can include a tapering of the aorta, dislocation of the tricuspid valve, and a number of conditions which restrict the amount of oxygen in the blood. These latter conditions that are characterized by cyanosis range from variations of the septal defect in the ventricle to dislocation of some of the larger blood vessels.

Peripheral Arterial Disease

Peripheral arterial disease or PAD is the gradual development over time of atherosclerotic plaques in the major arteries of the lower extremities. It is a very common disease and can result in a lack of blood flow to these areas. As a result, the most common symptoms are leg cramping and pain or actual discontinuous impaired gait, especially during exercise. Blood flow to the muscles is reduced and they become weakened over time. The mitochondria in the muscle cells generally cannot produce energy effectively. The likelihood of myocardial infarction, stroke, or death in these patients is high because their atherosclerosis is usually widespread throughout their vascular system.

Atrial Fibrillation

Atrial fibrillation is a type of dysrhythmia involving multiple waves of electrical impulses in the atrium. This results in an uneven response in the ventricles as well, plus a rapid and unsynchronized heart beat in the atrium as well as a decline in cardiac output. The goal of treatment is to reestablish a constant rhythm, especially the sinus rhythm, while attempting to prevent simultaneous blood clotting.

Restoration of a normal rhythm pattern, or cardioversion, is typically accomplished through the use of electrical shocks and/or by the use of drugs. Sometimes other techniques such as surgical tissue removal or insertion of implantable devices that control rhythm are performed. At the same time, low levels of anticoagulants such as warfarin are usually administered to prevent stroke without concomitant excessive bleeding.

Treatments

For individuals with valvular disease, it is important to thwart possible infection of the valve by administering antibiotics. If the disease becomes severe, then the valve may be replaced or repaired surgically. For patients with congestive heart failure, diuretics are typically given to relieve their fluid retention and the swelling in their lower extremities. In addition, individuals with CHF are given other drugs such as *B*-blockers or ACE inhibitors, and often more extreme measures are taken such as implantable devices for rhythm control, surgical restoration of the blood vessels, or even cardiac transplant. Lifestyle changes such as exercise are usually recommended for PAD patients but aspirin and other drug therapies are sometimes instituted as well.

Electrocardiogram

Typically there are 12 leads that can be placed at various areas on the body in an electrocardiogram (ECG). A rhythm strip is generated, which one can interpret in many ways. The first thing to look at is the heart rate to make sure it is within normal limits of 60 to 100 beats per minute. There are several portions to each repeating pattern which should be quantified. Certain abnormalities, if present, should be observed. These are reflected by a number of pattern changes and can indicate anything from enlarged heart compartments to electrical conduction problems to a heart attack. ECGs usually should be compared to previous tests and conclusions drawn.

Myocardial infarction, commonly known as a heart attack, occurs when the coronary artery is totally blocked. The result is actual necrosis or death of the affected area of the heart muscle. The most common abnormality on an ECG is initially an increase in the ST segment and peaking of the T waves. These alterations later return to pre-event levels but other changes in the Q or R waves can then develop. Since typically 12 different leads are connected when performing an ECG, the leads that show these changes indicate the region of the myocardial infarction. Skill in interpretation of the ECG is essential because other conditions can elicit changes in the ST segment, namely acute inflammation of the pericardial membrane and blockage of one of the bundle branches.

If patients are taking digitalis, a drug primarily used for CHF or arrhythmias in one of the atriums, there can be a delay in the electrical conduction. This causes ST segment and T wave abnormalities, which may be inaccurately interpreted as evidence of myocardial infarction during stress testing. When the left ventricle has become distended due to a condition called left ventricular hypertrophy, there is considerably more heart muscle than usual so the electrical conduction pattern is stressed and ECG changes are found. Typically, this disease shows a depression of the ST segment and other abnormalities. During exercise testing, if the pre-test baseline ST segment already shows some abnormal pattern, then interpretation of the ECG during exercise test monitoring is difficult.

Atrial Flutter

Atrial flutter is a variant of the re-entry type of tachydysrhythmia. Usually a blockage in the atrium occurs and the shunting of electrical conduction occurs, but only half of these waves are transmitted to the ventricle. Thus, the inferior ECG wires detect a zigzag-shaped rhythmic pattern where a high peak alternates with a lower peak. Approximately 300 of these flutter waves are observed every minute, and the beats per minute in the ventricle are elevated as well. This pattern is usually transient and the rhythm usually returns to normal or often fibrillation of the atrium instead.

Very Low Heart Rate

A very low heart rate, typically below 60 beats per minute, is usually due to some variation of sinus node dysfunction. The pacemaker effect that occurs at the sinoatrial node has been somehow compromised, although this condition does not necessarily indicate cardiac disease. The heart rate can be depressed by use of certain drugs or actually because an individual is so well-trained that their involuntary nervous responses are depressed. A low heart rate can, however, also indicate some problem with the SA node. In most of these cases, the regulation of electrical conduction is diverted to the atrioventricular junction, which cannot depolarize as quickly as the SA node, resulting in a lower heart rate and abnormal ECG patterns.

Atrioventricular Blocks

When electrical conduction is blocked at or below the atrioventricular node, atrioventricular blocks can occur. The simplest type of AV block involves a postponement of the induction in or between the atriums or at the AV junction region. In a second-degree block, there is actually some type of blockage either at the atrioventricular node or below it, which is indicated on an ECG by the eventual disappearance of P wave conduction to the ventricle. When the heart is completely blocked, waves cannot pass the atrioventricular junction area, so the atrium beats much faster than the ventricle.

Sinus Tachycardia

Sinus tachycardia is a type of dysrhythmia where the beat originating at the SA node is too fast, generally more than 100 beats per minute. This should be monitored during exercise testing or programs because it occurs as a result of any amplified action of the stress response as part of the sympathetic nervous system. The SA node responds to not only the voluntary nerves but also the involuntary nerves. If an individual is experiencing sinus tachycardia, their heart rate progressively, not abruptly, increases, sometimes up to their maximal rate.

Bundle Branch Blocks

A bundle branch block is a situation in which the electrical waves in the bundle branch region of either ventricle are obstructed. This results in non-synchronous firing in the other ventricle first. Thus, for example, in right bundle branch block, the left ventricle depolarizes first and vice versa for left bundle branch block. The most common electrocardiographic findings are wide QRS complexes, but ST segment elevation can also be found. Generally, only certain ECG leads show these changes. If bundle blocks occur, it is difficult to interpret ECG findings during exercise testing.

Exercise Testing

Exercise Training

Exercise training used as a physical fitness tool is aimed at improving cardiorespiratory fitness and muscular parameters. The regimens are based on two ideas. The first concept is that if a body component is stimulated to perform at previously unfamiliar levels, the functionality of that component will be increased. The second concept is that in general, training is specific for the activity or muscle group targeted. Thus, if the goal is overall fitness instead of just targeting a particular muscle group, then a range of exercises need to be incorporated into the program.

Typical Exercise Programs

The exercise physiologist or other professional typically designs an exercise program that is individualized for the subject. The goal is to incorporate activities that will hopefully become truly sustainable lifestyle changes in the individual. In addition, the program needs to be relatively safe yet enough to improve fitness. Therefore, there are usually four portions of the exercise program. The first is usually a 10 to 20 minute warm-up that slowly increases the resting metabolic rate to near the requirements in the next phase; low levels of activities to be performed in the next portion and perhaps some stretching are done. Then there is usually a longer conditioning phase in which endurance, strength and/or flexibility are targeted, perhaps in a rotating fashion on different days; in any case, the idea is to attain and keep the heart rate at 70 to 85% of its expected range. After that, a period which consists of some sort of enjoyable recreational pursuit might be incorporated. At the end, time to cool down with slower, less intense, or relaxing activities should be included as well as stretching.

During the conditioning phase of prescribed exercise, one goal is to improve the individual's cardiorespiratory fitness. This means improving their endurance in terms of increasing aerobic capacity and providing more oxygen to individual muscle groups. Thus, they may be able to exercise longer or do more repetitions of particular exercises. Responses are very individualized due to a variety of factors including genetic makeup, so even relatively low intensity exercises may provide some benefit, especially in initially unfit subjects.

Any activity that consumes oxygen and can be done in a constant and cadenced or repetitive fashion can be considered for the endurance phase of exercise prescription. Another concept for this phase is to incorporate use of a range of muscles. The activity should be performed for at least 20 minutes. Walking or some faster or machine-driven variation of it is often chosen as the primary exercise. A number of machines can be used if they use different muscle groups. More enjoyable activities such as dance or sports can be done if the individual has a minimum skill level or is not too competitive; these types of skill-based activities may be incorporated into a program at a later time.

Supervision of Exercise Testing

Various organizations including the American College of Cardiology and American Heart Association have outlined their recommendations about the supervision requirements for exercise testing. The consensus is that while physicians should be close and available if an emergency arises, the testing itself can usually be performed by a number of different types of trained professionals including the exercise physiologist. The healthcare professional should be familiar with a variety of cardiovascular and other signs, symptoms, and drugs and trained periodically in cardiopulmonary resuscitation. For high-risk subjects, the doctor should be in the room.

Consent Forms

Legally and ethically, a patient who may be undergoing exercise testing or participating in some type of program should be told verbally what is involved and also sign an informed consent form. These types of forms are used for other types of clinical trials as well, and if the exercise test is for experimental purposes, the Policy on Human Subjects for Research should be followed. Forms should contain wording explaining the scope of the test and its purpose, the possible risks involved, the participant's obligation to disclose health status information, and possible benefits. The individual should be told of their ability to withdraw from testing at any time, and they should willingly give their witnessed informed consent in writing.

Instructions

An individual who will be undergoing exercise testing should be told not to smoke, eat or drink alcohol or caffeine for at least 3 hours before the test. They should wear comfortable clothing and come relaxed to the site. They should bring a list of their medications and drink plenty of water. The issue of whether they remain on their medications prior to testing depends on a number of factors. If the exercise test is being performed just to simulate the subsequent exercise program, then they should keep taking their medications. If, on the other hand, the test is being performed in order to diagnose disease, the physician may ask them to taper or discontinue their cardiac medications for a few days before the test in order to get more accurate readings.

Field Tests

Field tests are a series of walking and running tests and their greatest advantage is that the only equipment required is a stopwatch. The most common current running tests measure the maximum distance covered in 12 minutes or they clock the time needed to cover 1.5 miles, but these may put sedentary or high-risk individuals at risk. One walking test measures heart rate toward the end of or immediately after a one mile walk. Another uses equations to predict peak oxygen consumption after a six minute walk. Maximal oxygen uptake can be predicted from all these tests. Their main disadvantage is that there is no way to monitor other things like blood pressure or heart rate during the actual test which can put the subject at risk.

Children and Adolescents

Children and younger adolescents generally have higher heart rates than adults, whether they are resting or performing exercise. Pediatric blood pressures are generally lower than those of adults, as are other measurements of cardiac output. Measurements of pulmonary function in terms of absolutes such the maximal oxygen output or the respiratory exchange ratio are lower for children than in adults, but equations taking into account the lower body weight and lack of efficiency during exercise of the child may give higher relative values such as oxygen uptake per kg body weight. These physiological variables return to resting rates much quicker in a child after they stop exercising.

Exercise Testing in Children

Children and adolescents often undergo routine assessments of their fitness level through their school or other organizations. Typically, this type of testing is limited to one or two tests each to evaluate cardiorespiratory stamina, muscular strength and endurance, and flexibility. Usually anthropometric measurements to estimate body composition are included. In addition, the incidence of actual clinical exercise testing is rather high in this population as well, and the tests are performed not only for reasons similar to those indicated in adults but also some others. Notable reasons to perform exercise testing in children and adolescents are adverse cardio or pulmonary reactions while participating in sports or to identify cardiac problems.

Exercise Testing in the Elderly

There are some unique issues that may need to be dealt with when performing an exercise test on an elderly subject. Many people in this age group have either neuromuscular problems such as difficulty balancing or orthopedic issues that restrict their ability to perform weight-bearing exercises. If the person has any of these problems, they may need to use a guardrail on the treadmill or the ergometer instead. Monitoring the individual during the test sometimes presents difficulty as well because the ECG during exercise in this population often indicates arrhythmias and has a decreased specificity so many false positives are recorded. Drugs the person is taking can affect not only the ECG but also blood profiles as well. For all of these reasons, generally the intensity of exercise is begun low and progresses slowly to higher levels.

Cardiorespiratory Exercise Program

In an older individual, generally exercise programs should be initially targeted at no more than 40 percent of their heart rate reserve or maximal oxygen uptake. It is suggested to actually record their maximal heart rate instead of estimating it from developed equations because this peak rate is so variable among individuals in this age range. Activities taking into account each individual's unique medical issues are incorporated so, for example, water or static bike exercises might be substituted for the more common walking. A target of a half hour of moderate movement a day is usually used but that exercise does not necessarily need to be done continuously. Some subjects can eventually progress to more intense workloads up to 3 days a week.

Physical Fitness Testing

A comfortable room is necessary during physical fitness testing, ideally close to 70 degrees Fahrenheit, with less than 60 percent humidity in the room, and with plenty of space per patient. All equipment to be used should be regularly calibrated monthly. The initial measurements to take at rest should be the heart rate and blood pressure and anthropometric calculations. Next, tests for cardiorespiratory endurance should be taken because some of these can produce dehydration if done first. Only after these are complete should muscular vigor tests be performed since they can raise the heart rate. Lastly, tests for flexibility are typically done.

Flexibility

Flexibility can be defined as the capacity of a particular joint to bend over a large range of motion. It is affected not only by the inherent properties of the underlying muscle and connecting tissues but it can increase upon warm-up as well. There are a number of devices to evaluate flexibility, all of which basically measure the angle of range of motion around the joint. These are known as goniometric measurements that utilize a giant protractor called a goniometer to measure the angle of maximum range of motion. Protractors to measure flexibility are also incorporated into handheld devices called inclinometers as well as isokinetic dynamometers. Depending on the joint being evaluated, the ability to flex and extend might be measured along with other joint-specific determinations.

Trunk Flexion Tests

There are two versions of trunk flexion tests, the Canadian Trunk Forward Flexion test, and the YMCA sit-and-reach test. The idea behind both tests is the same. The subject sits on the floor with feet either against a box called a flex meter in the Canadian test or heels at a yardstick mark for the YMCA version. The person leans forward slowly with parallel hands reaching as far as possible. The furthest point that the fingertips can reach is measured after holding this position for 2 seconds. The distance is compared to norms established for different age ranges and genders. Women can usually reach a little further than men in this case.

Indications for Exercise Testing

Exercise testing is generally utilized as a diagnostic tool in individuals who are either asymptomatic for CAD but who possess a number of risk factors for the disease or in people who are beginning an intense exercise protocol. In individuals who have or appear to have coronary artery disease, exercise testing becomes more of a prognostic tool in which a number of parameters can indicate how severe the disease might be. Several days after experiencing a heart attack, this testing might be done to assess the patient's post-MI treatment effectiveness and capability of performing daily activities upon release. Thus, there is a therapeutic component to the testing. Functional exercise testing, where values of METs are compared to normal values for age and gender using a nomogram, can serve to help healthcare professionals counsel and prescribe medications and recommendations to patients.

Submaximal Exercise Tests

There are two other types of submaximal exercise tests, treadmill tests and step tests. Calibrated treadmills are sometimes used with protocols similar in increasing intensity to the ergometer cycle with similar endpoints as long as each stage is at least 3 minutes. There are a few types of step tests as well in which typically a single step height is used at increasing work rates; sometimes a fixed work rate is kept. In any case, for these tests, heart rate is again measured and VO_{2max} is extrapolated from a nomogram. Some step tests, like the 3-Minute YMCA Step Test, offer a different approach in which the heart rate is measured immediately after a consistent height and rate stepping period and then evaluated more qualitatively from previous observations.

Less Than Maximal Exercise Testing

In many settings, particularly those geared more toward health and fitness and not done in a doctor's office, it is not feasible to have a setup for open-circuit spirometry. In addition, optimal exercise testing goes to the point of fatigue and may require a doctor or emergency intervention. However, the VO_{2max} can be predicted from the heart rate reaction to less than maximal workloads based on assumptions of uniformity of measurements and certain correlations between heart and work rate. It is important to make sure the individual is not taking heart medicines at the time of testing because they can change the heart rate.

Treadmill vs. Cycle Ergometer Testing

Individuals undergoing exercise testing are generally more familiar with the use of a treadmill (basically walking), than a cycle ergometer and therefore they will probably be able to demonstrate greater oxygen consumption and maximum heart rate on a treadmill. However, the fact that the individual is probably moving their arms and upper body parts during treadmill use can affect electrocardiogram and BP readings. On the other hand, the relative lack of familiarity with the cycle ergometer often results in less than optimal oxygen consumption readings and early termination of the testing. From a cost and portability perspective, the cycle is superior.

Exercise Test Protocols

Currently exercise protocols, whether employing the treadmill or cycle ergometer, either increase the workload in steps or continuously. One test where incremental increases are employed is the Bruce treadmill test; this protocol is best for young, healthy, or low-risk individuals because it uses fairly great differences between steps. There are several treadmill tests that utilize lesser incremental change which are more appropriate for older, sedentary, or higher risk people; these include the Naugton and Balke-Ware protocols. Ramp protocols employ an uninterrupted increase in the work during the treadmill or cycle ergometer test. The major advantages of these ramp protocols are that they can be individualized and that they provide consistent rises in responses and more accurate readings.

Upper Body Testing

There are arm cycle ergometers available, or they be made from regular stationary bicycles by changing out the pedals with handles and putting the cycle on a flat surface at shoulder level. The person being tested then sits and cranks usually at about 50 to 60 revolutions per minute and work rates are stepped up every few minutes. Measurements during testing require either careful timing or careful placement of ECG leads. For example, the thigh could be used to determine BP instead of the arm.

GXT Test

A GXT test is a graded exercise test, performed on either the treadmill or cycle ergometer, which takes into account the patient's symptoms. It is usually done to establish whether an individual can return to work after they have had some type of cardiac incident. Usually the GXT test measures the peak metabolic equivalent relative to the physical demands of their job. Functional testing may be appropriate as well if the individual's job requires a lot of muscular power, sporadic heavy work, or is performed in a hot setting.

Subjective Evaluations

Throughout clinical exercise testing, signs and symptoms should be monitored and recorded if found. In addition, subjects should be asked to provide what are called RPE, or ratings of perceived exertion, either toward the end of each workload cycle or every two minutes if they are on a Ramp regimen. The individual can signal responses manually by pointing if the testing apparatus prevents verbal communication. There are various scales that have been developed to grade these symptoms. The most important parameters to grade are evidence of chest pain, leg cramping, and difficulty breathing.

Exercise Stress Testing

The American College of Sports Medicine (ACSM) recommends exercise stress testing in individuals at moderate to high risk for cardiac events before they engage in vigorous exercise programs. According to the ACSM, individuals fall into these categories not only if they have diagnosed coronary disease or the presence of at least 2 risk factors for heart disease, but also because of their age. If a person wants to initiate an energetic exercise program over the age of 45 for men or 55 for women, exercise stress testing is advised.

Laboratory Tests

For individuals that are at low risk and appear to be healthy, a few laboratory tests should still be performed. The tests needed would be similar for people at moderate risk but without any obvious disease. These tests include a lipid panel following fasting, including all cholesterol values as well as triglycerides, and a blood glucose level after fasting as well. A screen of thyroid function is suggested too. High risk individuals need further laboratory tests as well. These additional laboratory tests include a range of other cardiac tests such as an electrocardiogram, tests to evaluate peripheral cardiac sites, and a chest radiograph for people with congestive heart failure. Further blood tests should be performed as well such as blood chemistries, CBCs, and various protein measurements.

Blood Pressure

Blood pressure (BP) measurements, particularly ones taken while seated, are extremely important because they have a direct correlation with the risk for cardiovascular problems and they can diagnose or predict hypertension. A normal individual typically has a systolic blood pressure of less than 120 mm Hg (mercury) and a diastolic blood pressure reading of less than 80 mm Hg. Values between 120-139 systolic and 80 to 89 mm Hg diastolic could be considered prehypertensive and drugs and healthy lifestyle changes are often suggested for individuals falling in this range, particularly if they have had diabetes, kidney disease or some cardiac event. Stage 1 hypertension is diagnosed with a BP in the range of 140-159 mm Hg during systole and 90-99 mm Hg during diastole. Drugs for hypertension and other issues would definitely be indicated for a BP in this range. Higher values indicate Stage 2 hypertension and at this point usually a combination of drugs would be given.

The most reliable measurement for resting blood pressure is taken with the patient seated in a supportive chair and their arm held at the height of their heart, but sometimes the BP may be taken with them lying on their back or standing. The upper arm is wrapped with the blood pressure cuff, again at the height of the heart. The healthcare provider places the stethoscope over the brachial artery and pumps up the pressure cuff 20 mm Hg higher than the first sound, whereby they begin to let out pressure slowly until they begin to hear what are called Korotkoff sounds. This point represents the systolic blood pressure, and when further pressure is released to the point where no sounds are heard, that is the diastolic pressure. Ideally, two or more readings separated by at least one minute should be taken.

Lipid and Lipoprotein Levels

Having elevated levels of low-density lipoprotein (LDL) cholesterol has been identified as a significant risk factor for predisposition to coronary artery disease and is the most important lipid measurement. Cholesterol lowering drugs are primarily aimed at this factor. In addition, a significant inverse relationship between CAD propensity and levels of high-density lipoprotein (HDL) cholesterol has also been suggested. Also, triglyceride levels appear to have a positive correlation with risk of coronary artery disease. Combining the unhealthy combination of these factors with abdominal obesity, elevated BP and some other factors is called "metabolic syndrome" and should be taken very seriously. Total cholesterol levels (desired value < 200) are usually taken as well and all measurements would be in mg/dL. Ideal LDL cholesterol, for example, would be less than 100 mg/dL; high (and therefore good) levels of HDL cholesterol are at least 60 mg/dL, and normal triglyceride levels are typically less than 150 mg/dL.

Duke Nomogram

The Duke nomogram consists of a series of 5 parallel lines that either measure or estimate by extrapolation parameters of exercise, evidence of coronary artery disease and prognosis. Initially, two measurements are observed during the exercise portion of the test, the deviation of the ST segment from at rest in millimeters, and the perceived absence or amount of angina. The points on these lines are joined and cross another line which assigns an ischemia reading. Then, the exercise capacity is plotted in metabolic equivalents and from that point another line is drawn to the ischemia reading line. The point of intersection on a fifth line representing prognosis can estimate the likelihood the individual may die from or survive CAD.

Exercise Prescription

Physical Activity Recommendations

The guidelines for recommended physical activity levels are different depending on the reports quoted. The Surgeon General's Report, Physical Activity and Health, suggests health can be enhanced by moderate physical activity most days of the week. For the purposes of that report, moderate activity would be something like 30 minutes of fast walking. Several other current reports which emphasized energy balance have recommended more physical activity than the Surgeon General's Report. The focus of these reports was more on weight maintenance and loss, but they also conclude that the moderate activity levels are enough to provide numerous health benefits, particularly in reducing risk of cardiovascular disease.

Training Terminology

Isometric resistance training is a way of developing muscle in which the muscle is held against a force in one position without moving. The most improvements in the muscle performance will be when the muscle is in the position that the training was done. Proper breathing is essential in this type of training. A *core exercise* is one that uses more than one muscle group and joint, such as squats. *Core training* is a program of exercise in which the muscles of the abdomen and back are the focus. Focusing also on muscles that attach to the torso will help to prevent injury. *Balance* is being able to stay in one place for an extended time. *Plyometric training* is a program of exercise in which a resistance is combined with a quick movement, thereby combining strength training with speed development.

Stages of Progression

Progression is the concept of increasing the level of activity through three stages in order to eventually reach the point when the person sustains a satisfactory level of fitness over time.

- The *initial conditioning stage* is when a person begins exercising. Exercise programs at this stage should be attainable and motivating, and include a significant period of warming up the muscles, lower intensity activities and a significant period of cooling down the muscles. Exercise may initially be scheduled for as little as 12 minutes, 3 days per week, with an increase over time.
- The *improvement stage* is the stage in which the person is well motivated by the initial success. Exercise should increase in how hard it is, and how long and how often it is performed.
- The *maintenance stage* is the final stage when the person begins to sustain fitness over time.

Steps in Exercise Prescription

The first step in actual exercise prescription is to assess the type of training effect desired which is really determined by the goal of the program and the fitness level of the individual. Subsequently, the desired maximal oxygen consumption range is calculated as a percentage of the difference between maximum and resting VO_2, that is: desired oxygen uptake = (number of MET's theoretically achievable - resting at 3.5 mL per kilogram per minute) x percent desired. Then, equations have been developed for common endurance exercises that relate the typical oxygen consumption for that activity relative to other parameters. For example, equations for walking or running on the treadmill compare the oxygen consumption to speed and percent grade. Limb ergometer work correlates oxygen uptake with work rates and body mass. Equations describing the use of step machines relate the number of steps per minute and height in meters to the desired oxygen uptake.

Muscle Actions

An *isometric action* is stable and unmoving. The joint does not move and the muscle does not change in length. Isometric exercise will result in added strength only in the exact position the action was held. An *isokinetic action* is a motion made on a machine that controls the speed and force of the movement. An *isotonic (dynamic) action* moves visibly, and is the action most often associated with standard muscle training. The two types of isotonic actions are:

- Concentric action (or positive contraction), which is a motion of the muscle as it works against a resistance that results in a shorter muscle
- Eccentric action (or negative contraction), which is a motion of the muscle as it lengthens against a resistance.

Warm-Up

There are a few different reasons why every workout should begin with a warm up session. For one thing, it is healthier for the heart to have a gradual introduction to exercise. If the heart is asked to go from a state of rest to a state of major exertion, it may have a hard time. In general, it is a good idea for the warm-up period to raise the temperature by a couple of degrees, as this will create better circulation. When the flow of blood through the body increases, the muscles receive more nutrients and are more prepared for the increased needs of the workout. The warm-up period also gives the joints and tendons a chance to limber up before more serious exertion. The movements made during the warm-up period should resemble those that will be made during the core of the work-out, so that the right parts of the body will be prepared.

Cool-Down

The third and final part of a basic work-out is the cool-down period. This is the period in which exertion decreases and the focus is on gradually slowing down in order to preserve flexibility and range of motion. Studies of human physiology have revealed that the cool-down period serves a distinct purpose in a work-out.

Instruction Strategies

<u>Command style</u> -- One of the common kinds of instruction used in fitness classes is known as the command style. In the command style of instruction, the instructor

makes all decisions about exercise program. The participants in the class have no input into the content or pace of the class. One of the problems with the command style is that it is very difficult to adjust the intensity according to the particular needs of individuals within the class. Teachers who use the command style are likely to find that individuals at the extremes of a fitness range are not satisfied. One advantage of the command style of instruction is that it allows the instructor to maintain control over the class and monitor safety issues closely.

Slow-to-fast strategy -- One of the strategies used by fitness instructors for teaching complicated exercise routines is known as the slow to fast strategy. Instructors who use this strategy start a new routine very slowly, and gradually increase speed as the participants in the class move from cognitive understanding, to associative understanding, and finally to autonomous understanding. Common sense suggests that individuals will be better able to make self-corrections when they learn a new maneuver slowly. One consideration to take into account when using the slow-to-fast strategy is that it will immediately decrease the intensity of the exercise, and so is probably inappropriate for the peak times in the exercise class. For this reason, many instructors use the slow to fast strategy to teach new maneuvers at the beginning of each class.

Practice style -- One of the common styles of instruction used by fitness teachers is known as the practice style. Instructors who use the practice style give their participants a great deal of freedom to make adjustments during the exercise class. The instructor will circulate throughout the room providing personalized feedback to the participants, and the participants will be allowed to adjust the intensity and quantity of their exercise. This technique is good when all the participants in the class have moderate experience in the fitness training, and are capable of judging their own performance. The practice style of instruction is not appropriate for beginning classes.

Reciprocal style -- One of the common styles of instruction used by fitness teachers is the reciprocal style. This style of instruction is useful when the participants in the fitness class are too numerous to be given personalized feedback. In the reciprocal style of instruction, the participants in the class are divided into pairs, and instructed to monitor and provide feedback to one another. A fitness instructor should take care not to place inexperienced members of the class in partnerships with one another. Also, the fitness instructor should provide specific instruction to the participants as to what they should be looking for in their partner's performance.

Self-check style -- One of the common styles of instruction used by fitness teachers is the self-check style. In this style of teaching, the instructor has all the participants in the class monitor their own progress. This may involve checking heart rate, recording measurements, or filling out some brief documentation. This kind of instruction is especially effective during exercises that can be easily measured, as for instance muscular strength and endurance training exercises, and cardiorespiratory exercises. The self-check style of instruction should only be used when all the participants in the class are experienced.

Inclusion style -- When the participants in an exercise class represent a wide range of fitness levels, the instructor may want to incorporate the inclusion style of instruction. The instructor who uses the inclusion style demonstrates an array of different techniques and activities that can be performed by individuals at different fitness levels. One example of this kind of instruction is the presentation of alternative stretches for those individuals who cannot perform the basic stretches that have been taught. The inclusion style of instruction is necessary when the class has a particularly broad range of fitness levels. It is time consuming, however, and so should not be used unless it is absolutely necessary.

Strategies for Teaching Movement

Repetition reduction strategy -- One of the common instruction strategies used in exercise classes is known as the repetition reduction strategy. To use this strategy, the instructor simply increases the number of repetitions by two or three times. For instance, an aerobics instructor who is trying to teach a pattern of two steps forward and one kick left might first teach a pattern of four steps forward and two kicks last. This teaching strategy helps the participants in the class to achieve a quick cognitive understanding of the move. The repetition reduction strategy is most effective when it is set to music.

Spatial strategy -- One of the common instruction strategies used in exercise classes is known as the spatial strategy. A teacher using this strategy will explain the proper technique for a maneuver one body part at a time. In other words, when describing an elaborate dance sequence, a teacher would begin by describing the movement of the right foot and leg, then the left foot and leg, and then the left and right arms, respectively. A teacher using the spatial strategy may have participants in the class practice the movements of one part of the body in isolation before moving on to other parts. Many teachers of complex exercise routines find that the spatial strategy helps students to gradually assimilate a complicated maneuver. Instructors may either work from the bottom of the body up or from the top down.

Part-to-whole strategy -- One of the common teaching strategies employed by fitness instructors for teaching complex movements is called the part-to-whole strategy. A teacher using the part-to-whole strategy will break a complicated move down into simple parts which can be taught independently. After the first part of the move has been mastered, the class can move on to the second part, and so on. By building knowledge incrementally, the teacher maintains the confidence of the class and ensures that each component of the complex maneuver is performed correctly. This strategy for instruction is especially effective with beginning level classes.

Simple-to-complex strategy -- One of the common instructional strategies used by fitness instructors when teaching complex movements is known as the simple-to-complex teaching strategy. This strategy simply consists of beginning with the simplest parts of a complex maneuver, and gradually increasing the complexity. For example, an instructor teaching dance moves that requires elaborate gestures with both arms might begin by instructing the participants in the movements of only one arm. After the participants have mastered the movements of the right arm, say, they can begin to learn the movements for the left arm.

Training Systems

Pyramid system -- involves increasing or decreasing weights and repetitions in one raining session. An ascending pyramid system involves lifting more weight while decreasing the number of times the weight is lifted. A descending pyramid involves starting with the most weight the person can lift at one time, and then lifting less weight more times with each set. The complete pyramid system is a combination of these two systems, lifting more weight fewer times until the person reaches his maximum weight, and then lifting less weight more times.

Super-slow training system -- involves doing an activity very slowly, pausing at the peak of the resistance, and then returning very slowly.

Cheat system-- involves doing an activity correctly until the muscles are completely exhausted, then doing the activity incorrectly a few more times, allowing gravity or other muscles to complete the activity. This has a high risk of injury.

Pre-exhaustion system -- involves doing activities that use bigger muscle sets before activities that use big and small muscle sets. Smaller muscles will tire before bigger muscles, so if the bigger muscles are not somewhat tired before doing the combined activity, the person will have to stop lifting when the smaller muscles get tired and the bigger muscles will not work to their maximum capacity. If the muscles do not work to maximum capacity, they cannot be overloaded, and improvements in strength are not likely.

Priority training--focuses on working smaller, less strong muscles at the beginning of an exercise session.

Split routine system-- alternates working muscle groups on different days so that the person works out every day, but some muscles will rest on any given day. The blitz system is similar to a split routine, but each session focuses on only one particular part of the body.

Circuit training -- involves moving from one activity to another without a break. The person does one set of each activity with moderate vigor.

Super-circuit training -- involves alternating weight training with cardiovascular exercises.

Partial repetitions system (or "burn system") -- involves the person working as hard as she can in complete motion activities, then doing variations of those activities while only partially completing the movement.

Forced repetitions system -- involves the person working as hard as she can on an activity, then a physiologist steps in to help her repeat the activity a few more times.

Eccentric training (or "negative training") -- involves working opposing muscle groups harder. Either a special machine increases the weight on the return (eccentric) part of the activity, or the physiologist will help the person lift the weight on the main part of the activity, then let go for the return part.

Monitoring Intensity and Frequency

In order to provide fitness instruction at the appropriate level of intensity to all the members of the class, the instructor needs to closely monitor the intensity of each participant. Instructor should be aware that most participants in an exercise class will be at a lower level of fitness than the instructor himself or herself. Keeping this in mind, the instructor should slow down to the level of the participants. Participants should always be capable of measuring their own heart rate. Individuals should not be allowed to participate in too many exercise classes in a given week. This is because the body needs sufficient recovery time between high-intensity workouts.

Safety Issues

In order to keep an exercise class safe and effective, an instructor needs to teach in small concise steps. In other words, the participants in the class should not be told to perform a complex series of movements before they have fully understood the process. In addition, the intensity level of the exercise should be kept at a moderate level until participants have fully learned the sequence. The instructor should be careful to circulate throughout the room monitoring the performance of all the participants in the class. Special attention should be paid to the posture and spinal alignment of each participant, as errors in posture can often lead to serious back injury.

Planning Ahead

Many fitness instructors make the mistake of trying to plan their exercise programs on the fly. By planning ahead, the instructor will be more likely to select activities that efficiently lead the class towards the exercise goals. Indeed, the beginning point of the planning process should be the fitness objectives of the class. For instance, if a class has set as a goal the improvement of flexibility, the instructor will want to select activities that are geared towards this goal. If the goal of the class is to improve cardiorespiratory endurance, the instructor may want to extend the period of high intensity aerobic exercise, possibly by diminishing the duration of muscular strength exercises.

Training Program Set-Up

Proper floor or surface -- Before developing a fitness program, instructor should take into account the quality of the floor in the fitness room. The floor of the exercise room needs to be sufficiently springy to absorb shocks of running and jumping. Also, the floor needs to provide enough traction so that the participants in the class can move around without being at risk of slipping and falling. Hardwood floors are good for exercising, as long as there is sufficient padding underneath. Some carpets are appropriate for exercise classes, as long as the fringe is not too long. Exercise classes may be conducted outdoors, as long as the grass is not too long and the surface is not too uneven.

Proper equipment -- In order to be effective, physical fitness equipment must be used according to certain basic rules. A fitness instructor should regularly check equipment for signs of wear and tear. Fitness equipment should only be used for the purpose for which it was designed. Before beginning a section of the fitness class in which the equipment is to be used, the instructor should make sure that all the participants are familiar with its operation. As participants in the class begin to use the fitness equipment, the instructor should circulate throughout the room and monitor the participants to make sure that safety guidelines are being followed.

Before the initiation of an exercise program, the instructor should make sure that all the appropriate equipment is available. Floor exercises will require some kind of mat, while strength enhancement exercises will probably involve some kind of resistance training equipment. Other common needs during aerobic classes are jump ropes, steps, and Swedish balls. The instructor should know how to use all the necessary equipment for the class. Finally, the instructor wants to play music during the class, he or she should make sure that a stereo system is present.

Exercise class area -- Fitness instructors should take special care in the arrangement of participants during exercise class. The most common arrangement is to have the participants standing or sitting in rows. This is perhaps the most effective way to fit a large number of students into a short area, but it may prevent the instructor from seeing participants in the back of the classroom. This is especially problematic when the most experienced and fit members of the class cluster towards the front, near the instructor. If this becomes a problem, the instructor should take special care to circulate throughout the room during the exercise class. If possible, the instructor may want to place the members of the class in a circle or semicircle. One problem with these arrangements, however, is that they force the members of the class to look directly at one another. Self-conscious members of an exercise class may be uncomfortable with this arrangement.

Exercise facility -- An ideal exercise facility should be well ventilated and neither too hot nor too cold. Most experts agree that the appropriate temperature for an exercise class is around 70° Fahrenheit. The floor of the exercise facility should be springy enough to cushion the impact of intense exercise, but not so bouncy that it will diminish the balance of the participants. Many exercise classes are equipped with mirrors on all the walls, so that the participants can monitor their own performance during the class. It may be helpful for the instructor to stand on a dais, or raised platform, so that he or she can be seen by all the participants in the class. Finally, it is essential that the participants in the class have access to water at all times; many exercise facilities have water fountains within the room.

Exercise Adherence

Exercise program -- There are a number of aspects of an exercise program that can affect adherence by the participants. Some individuals will be less likely to attend a fitness class that occurs at a certain time of day, for instance after lunch or early in the morning. Some participants will not be able to regularly attend classes that last longer than an hour. Also, some participants will be unlikely to attend a class if they feel that they are either too fit or not fit enough. In order to encourage adherence to the exercise plan, a fitness instructor should be familiar with the personal needs and fitness requirements of all the individuals in the class.

Environmental factors -- There are a number of environmental factors that may affect the appearance of the participants in an exercise class to the fitness plan. An exercise room that is clean and bright will encourage participants to return. If the room is too cold or hot, participants will be less likely to come back. Perhaps the most important aspect of the fitness environment, though, is the rapport between the fitness instructor and the participants. Instructors who are supportive and positive with their students tend to have higher levels of adherence. Instructors should always be professional and punctual to their classes, so as to encourage similar virtues in the students.

Cardiorespiratory Conditioning

Cardiorespiratory conditioning is simply activity that aims to improve the health of the heart and lungs. Individuals engaging in cardiorespiratory conditioning should gradually increase the intensity of their exertion, to avoid putting a sudden and violent strain on the heart or lungs. There are many different activities that qualify as cardiorespiratory conditioning. Basically, any activity that brings the individual close to his or her target heart rate can be considered cardiorespiratory conditioning. An effective conditioning session will work all of the major muscle groups. Many fitness instructors incorporate music into their cardiorespiratory programs.

Muscle Conditioning

Every person needs a basic amount of muscle conditioning in order to perform everyday activities. Although muscle conditioning exercises are often associated with bodybuilding in the development of large muscle mass, they actually are a good idea for individuals of all ages and fitness levels. In order to make a muscle conditioning class effective, though, the instructor needs to develop a program that works complementary muscle groups. When large weights are being used, the instructor needs to pay particular attention to proper technique as the risk of injury is elevated. Finally, instructor should be familiar with the specific fitness goals of each participant so that he or she can focus the exercise program on balance, muscular strength, muscular development and flexibility as necessary.

Core Region Strengthening Exercises

The two main types of exercise programs that primarily target strengthening the muscles in the middle or core region are Pilates exercises and use of the stability ball as a tool. The underlying concept of both programs is that if an individual is strong in their core torso region, other parts of the body will be more effectively utilized. The stability ball enhances muscular strength by virtue of its instability which forces the person to recruit many muscles to maintain balance, and core strength because that is the area around which most of the exercises have been structured. Pilates, named after its developer Joseph Pilates, incorporates a vast array of mat and machine-based exercises that are centered on the basic principles of steady, carefully regulated movements, proper breathing techniques, and optimal range of motion. The actual exercises are always begun from the core thus serving to strengthen that region.

Exercise Intensity

Calculating the intensity of an exercise is sometimes based on a proportion of the individual's maximal oxygen uptake. Currently, this calculation is less often used than heart rate methods or subjective measurements because it is very hard to pinpoint the caloric requirements based on this parameter alone. If the VO_{2max} is used to determine an intended intensity based on oxygen uptake, the targeted oxygen uptake (VO_2 level in mL per kg per minute) is generally 60 to 80 percent of the estimated peak, although it may be considerably less for extremely unfit individuals. To calculate this target VO_2, the resting oxygen uptake is added to the product of the difference between maximal and resting oxygen uptake and the desired percent intensity level.

Energy Expenditure

During exercise, the rate of energy metabolism in the muscles is highly elevated compared to more sedentary activities. There are both aerobic and anaerobic components in this metabolism, which means oxygen is or is not involved. During short (and usually concentrated) bouts of exercise, the metabolic pathways shift more toward anaerobic energy creation. Adenosine triphosphate (ATP) is the substrate needed to produce energy for muscle contractions because it is constantly being converted into energy production plus formation of adenosine diphosphate (ADP) and inorganic phosphate. In turn, one mechanism of utilizing this ADP is for it to accept a phosphate from creatine phosphate reforming ATP and creatine; this occurs often during brief, intense exercise and is anaerobic. In addition, during this type of exercise session, carbohydrates are utilized to produce energy by generating ATP molecules at various points in a process called glycolysis. Depending on the substance being broken down, glucose or glycogen, the number of ATPs generated is 2 or 3. This latter pathway again does not use oxygen but it can lead to aerobic ATP generation at one of the later steps where pyruvate has been formed.

Generally, when an exercise session is longer than about a half hour, the individual is participating in a less intense workload. This shifts the energy metabolism involved in muscle contraction toward mechanisms involving oxygen. In addition, fat and sometimes protein, not just carbohydrates, are utilized. During prolonged exercise, the pyruvic acid that was generated by glycolysis enters the mitochondrion of the cell where it is utilized in an aerobic process called oxidative phosphorylation.

Basically, oxidative phosphorylation is the combined term for the generation of ATP by two different mechanisms. The first, known as the Krebs cycle, extracts hydrogen from various molecules, and then the electron transport chain uses the energy produced to ultimately add a phosphate to ADP to generate ATP and water. Fat can also be aerobically utilized in the mitochondria to produce ATPs by being converted to acetyl-CoA, which is also a substrate for the above processes.

Group Cardiovascular Workout

When an exercise professional leads a group cardiovascular workout class, there are basically three types of programs that they might use or mix. In the first, some objective is desired such as achieving a particular heart rate or perceived difficulty; once that goal is achieved, the session is designed to maintain that parameter throughout the remainder of the time period. Commonly a type of programming called interval training is used in which after minimal aerobic warm-up periods of high and low or moderate workloads are alternated while maintaining some level of activity throughout. Here, the proportion of high workload to the less intense recovery period can be modified according to the type of class attendees. The third type of cardiovascular workout incorporates a sequence of exercises that may use some equipment, each part is designed to serve a particular purpose, and aerobics may be interspersed. This last type, circuit training, typically involves moving around the room to different locations at the instructors signal.

Muscular Strengthening Group Exercises

In a group setting, exercise programs usually use the muscular strengthening portion to increase muscular stamina. This is usually done not by using the larger machines (since there are not enough) but by employing simpler resistances like elastic tubes or dumbbells in a repetitive fashion. Different exercises are done for all the major muscle groups, unless a preexisting condition suggests otherwise. Newer concepts suggest a progressive system where initially the individual concentrates on learning how to isolate a particular muscle group while lying down before additional forces are added or their stance changes. Eventually more resistance is added. If the individual can handle it, ultimately more intricate exercises that combine muscle groups or add other components such as ability to balance are added as well. Sometimes programs are designed to incorporate exercises that may improve daily life or enhance sports performance.

Cardiorespiratory Exercise Intensity

The heart and lungs need time to adjust to the increased workload during exercise. When the body is in a state of rest, the majority of the blood tends to concentrate in the internal organs. When the peripheral muscles begin to work however, more blood is required in the outlying parts of the body, and the heart needs time to meet these demands. At the same time, the respiratory system will need to increase its speed in order to deliver oxygen to the muscles. Otherwise, the elevated circulation of the blood throughout the body will be ineffective because it will not contain enough oxygen. For this reason, exercise programs should begin slowly and only increase in intensity gradually, so that the heart and lungs will have time to adjust to their increased workload.

Basic Standing Stretches

Most exercise classes contain some basic flexibility exercises at either the beginning or the end. There are four basic stretches that are performed from a standing position. The hamstring stretch, the individual extends one leg in front of the other and leans forward, such that the extended leg is bent. The gastrocnemius muscle can be stretched in this same position, by leaning forward over the front foot. By then leaning backward and bending the back knee, the soleus is stretched. In this position, the shoulder extensors can be stretched by reaching up and back with the hands pressed together.

Cooling Down Period

A cooling down period where very slow movements and stretches are performed at the end of an exercise session is very important. The reason is that the extremities may develop edema from blood accumulation if this is not done. Normal blood pressures need to be restored during this portion. In addition, this section usually is designed to improve the suppleness of the joints with a variety of stretches and sometimes restore the individual's peace of mind by using relaxation techniques such as yoga. This final portion of the workout should last up to about 10 minutes.

Mixed-Impact Aerobics

"Mixed-impact" aerobics means that oxygen consuming exercises placing a lot of pressure on the legs are interspersed with those of lesser impact. This type of class is usually accompanied by music which may set the tone for each exercise. Accommodations or modifications of the higher impact exercises can allow each participant to go at their own pace. Typically, these classes include periodic checking of one's pulse or fatigue level. As with any program, adequate hydration, footwear, and cooling down periods are especially important for these types of classes.

Step Classes

Step classes are designed to improve cardiopulmonary parameters without putting high stress on the lower extremities, as may be the case with an aerobics class. They involve stepping up and down or lunging off platforms on the floor alternating with stepping in place, usually to music. Workload is most effectively controlled by the height of the step, not the speed of music or use of additional weights. In fact, because a combination of motor skills is required to perform step training, it is important not to do the exercises too fast, especially for beginners. Footwear and proper stepping techniques are very important. Proper technique encompasses things like using the whole foot, standing tall, and bending from the knees when changing positions.

Martial Arts Classes

Martial arts classes as utilized in a group exercise setting today are mainly aerobic in nature in which kicks and other moves from martial arts are alternated with other aerobic components like walking. The main concern with these programs is that the instructor really needs to be well-trained in the martial arts so that proper technique is taught. Another major issue is the adherence to the use of exercises that do not go beyond the normal range of motion. Correct stance, with toes turned out and knees loose, must be emphasized for maintenance of stability and joint health. Martial arts classes need to be approached as a gradual goal which supplements other forms of training.

Water Exercises

Water is a good medium in which to perform exercises for many people. The basic reason is that it reduces or virtually eliminates the weight-bearing component of the exercise. Thus, water reduces risk of injury to the lower portions of the body while providing its own resistance component. This makes it ideal for people with low blood flow. Typically, water exercises done in the shallow end of the pool often do put a little stress on the lower extremities, such as hopping, and may be unsuitable for certain people. If the group cannot touch the pool floor, that is considered deep water fitness, and is actually safer in many ways. In this case, the individual always uses some type of floatation device which eliminates the weight-bearing component, forces them to practice good posture, promotes good balance, and may increase their range of motion. Other equipment can be added to amplify the resisting forces. The emphasis is generally on doing exercises that simultaneously activate a number of muscle groups.

Indoor Cycling

Indoor cycling programs are generally structured to in some way simulate riding a bicycle outdoors, including imagined changes of terrain and intensity. An advantage of cycling is that it does not bear weight on the lower body. The teacher prompts the changes verbally which in theory should encourage those in the class to change their speed or resistance or the manner in which they ride the bicycle in response to the images invoked. The faster the individual peddles, the less resistance they encounter, and vice versa. Proper technique is crucial, with the knee never coming above the hip in the up position and almost straight in the down position. Proper footwear and non-chafing shorts should be worn. Theoretically, the attendee self-pace themselves with indoor cycling but this type of program does tax the lower extremities in terms of muscle and other tissue use and does put stress on the cardiopulmonary system.

Oxygen Consumption and Heart Rate

Oxygen consumption and heart rate are directly related. Use of HR to set the guidelines for exercise intensity is often preferred because it is more easily measured. When this parameter is used, the objective is to keep the heart rate near the middle of the desired range. For high-risk or unfit individuals, the direct method of calculating the desired heart rate is often used; for this technique, the heart rate is plotted on a xy plot, versus either the oxygen uptake or exercise intensity, and then the desired HR is set in the range desired. Another calculation utilizes the percentage of maximal heart rate desired, but it is not very precise, especially at low workloads. The targeted heart rate reserve method employs a calculation that is very similar to determining the targeted oxygen uptake; the resting heart rate is added to the product of the difference between maximal and resting heart rate and the desired percent intensity level.

RPE Scales

RPE scales are subjective ratings that have been developed as guidelines for the subject to evaluate or rate their perceived exertion levels. If a patient is taking medication, sometimes the RPE is useful because the other measurements can be changed by the drug. Such subjective measurements can be affected by many factors including the exercise modality used and individual perceptions. They correlate only roughly with heart rate measurements. Nevertheless, determining some sort of target perceived exertion level as an adjunct evaluation during the training is useful.

Duration and Frequency

For most people, the endurance phase of exercise protocols to improve cardiorespiratory fitness, including maximal oxygen uptake, should be about 20 to 30 minutes of intermediate workload. There is some limited data to support the ideas that other combinations that are either one or several short periods a day of highly intense exercise or conversely a low workload but longer duration protocol can be effective. Very unfit individuals might start with multiple very short duration periods interspersed with resting. The recommended frequency of exercise is generally 3 to 5 days a week. The major exceptions would be very unfit individuals who should exercise for a short period every day, or athletes who might exercise up to 6 days a week.

Resistance Training

Actually, resistance or weight training may slightly improve cardiorespiratory fitness, but this type of training does not correlate well with heart rate measurements or an increase in maximal oxygen consumption. Weight training expends only a minimal amount of calories during work, rest, and for a couple hours after termination. The typical caloric expenditure is up to 10 kilocalories per minute at the most. Aerobic activities burn up many more calories than resistance protocols do.

The major goals in resistance training programs are to promote and sustain muscular strength and endurance and to shift the body composition toward more fat-free or lean body mass (LBM). Determining the workload and number of repetitions to be performed is very subjective. The difficulty of the resistance protocol is basically evaluated by how fatigued the muscle becomes relative to at rest. The number of repetitions that one can perform before the muscle fails is the repetition maximum or RM. Protocols could be either a low number of repetitions at high workloads or more times at lesser resistance levels. The issue of shifting to LBM is important because the metabolic rate at rest may be increased with proportionately greater lean body mass; unfortunately, this goal is often unachievable. During resistance training, more muscle fibers typically become involved as the number of repetitions increases toward fatigue. A spike in blood pressure proportional to the number of muscle fibers involved occurs as well. For relatively healthy subjects, this momentary blood pressure spike is probably not detrimental. However, for anyone at risk following an increase in their blood pressure such as hypertensive individuals, resistance training may be inappropriate or should be done at low workload levels and stopped before the muscle group fails.

Most weight training protocols for vigorous individuals use about an 8 to 12 RM done at relatively high or maximal workloads for ideal muscular fatigue. Regimens which employ fewer repetitions at high intensity have been correlated with enhancement of bone mineral density. Thus, the most significant group of people that might use these types of protocols are those predisposed to osteoporosis, most-notably postmenopausal or other women or the elderly in general.

Heightening Workload

Muscle groups are specific in purpose. Nevertheless, different target exercises can increase intensity, most notably by increasing the length to the pivot point. A variety of muscle groups should be targeted. The healthcare professional can try increasing the weight lifted or the number of times the weight is elevated in the sequence. If the movement is slowed down, difficulty is increased. If the entire series of repetitions are performed without stopping, the intensity is heightened. There has been some suggestion that performing two sets of each exercise in the regimen is useful relative to just one set, but this has not been well-studied.

Stretching Exercises

Stretching is a transient method of increasing flexibility. It involves increasing the range of motion (ROM) around various joints by methodically lengthening the muscles and tendons at the site that are restricting the ROM. These exercises rely on the principles that muscles do have elastic properties as well as the ability to lengthen with applied force. Most safely performed stretching exercises are static, which means that they only involve stretching the muscle until it feels tight and then holding it there up to about a half minute. Only a few repetitions of all types of stretches are needed, and if the muscles are warm, the stretching is easier. Flexibility exercises should be done several times a week, preferably daily.

Maintaining Effects

Use of exercises at the maximum intensity or workload is necessary to sustain the effects of training, whether they are aerobic activities like jogging or resistance training. The frequency or length of time involved can be lowered without appreciable loss of fitness in terms of VO_{2max} as long as the ultimate level of intensity is still used. If individuals stop training altogether, they will lose some of the training effect within the first few weeks; the prior training time is directly related to the time until loss of the training effect. Therefore, maintenance can occur as long as some exercise at maximum workload is routinely done.

SUPERVISION

Most people can actually engage in an exercise program safely without direct supervision. However, individuals belonging to a high risk group should be supervised by appropriately trained personnel under the direction of a doctor; this includes anyone presenting with any sign or symptom of cardiovascular, metabolic, or pulmonary disease and anyone known by history to have any of these disorders. If the subject falls either into the moderate risk category or is being well-managed, the doctor's presence is not essential. Often a low capacity to consume oxygen alone can dictate use of supervising personnel; this is true for anyone with METs of less than 7 mL per kg per minute.

MOTIVATION

Unfortunately, many individuals will be unable to stick with an exercise program over a long period of time. In order to minimize the number of dropouts, a fitness instructor needs to know how to maintain high motivation in the class participants. One sure way to discourage the participants in the class is by setting unrealistic expectations. The goals for the class should be challenging but realistic. At all times, the instructor should be reminding the participants of the positive benefits of exercise, especially those that are not visible to the naked eye. Although it is inevitable that some of the fitness work will be strenuous and difficult, as much as possible, the instructor should endeavor to make classes fun.

<u>Setting exercise goals</u> -- One of the most effective ways to maintain motivation in the participants in an exercise class is by setting challenging and realistic goals. These goals should be created by the fitness instructor in consultation with each participant. Individuals may have short and long term goals regarding muscular strength, endurance, flexibility, and weight loss. The fitness goals should always be written down and reviewed regularly. Some of the short-term goals that many participants in an exercise class have are to be able to achieve a complicated dance sequence, to endure high-intensity cardiorespiratory exercise for a longer period of time, or to demonstrate increased flexibility.

<u>Giving regular, positive feedback</u> -- One of the most important things a fitness instructor can do is to provide positive feedback and reinforcement to all the participants in the class. Studies indicate that students consistently perform better when they are given continual encouragement. It is important, however, that the praise given by the instructor be specific. To this end, the instructor should maintain detailed records of performance. This way, the instructor will be able to point out specific areas in which each participant has improved. It is common for participants to become discouraged and forget how much progress they have made during the course of an exercise program. The job of the instructor is to remind each participant of long-term goals and progress.

Making exercise sessions enjoyable – The fitness instructor should never discourage participants by making the exercise class too difficult, boring, or complicated. Instead, the instructor should maintain a positive environment atmosphere in the class. To make sure that the class environment is acceptable for all the participants in the class, the instructor should regularly confer with the participants on possible music and variations in the exercise program. Students will be more enthusiastic about an exercise class in which they feel they have an influence. The instructor should regularly ask for feedback from the participants, for instance on which areas of the class are considered to be successful and which are less effective. Finally, the instructor should endeavor to maintain a positive attitude as much as possible.

Acknowledging the discomforts of exercise -- Although the fitness instructor should seek to minimize discomfort for participants during an exercise class, it is to be expected that there will be some degree of discomfort during strenuous exercise. A fitness instructor needs to be able to distinguish between normal levels of pain and pain that may indicate injury. A fitness instructor should take seriously any complaints of pain made by the participants. However, a fitness instructor should make sure that that all participants can distinguish between signs of serious health problems and the normal results of vigorous exercise. Any participants who complain of chest pain, dizziness, or lightheadedness should immediately decrease intensity.

Using cues and reminders -- Many fitness instructors find that they can increase adherence to an exercise program by using cues and reminders. An example of such a reminder might be a regular newsletter detailing the activities of the class, or a flyer posted at the exercise facility. A fitness instructor might make copies of the music used during the fitness class, so that participants can remind themselves of the fitness environment while at home or at work.

Encouraging social supports -- One way that many fitness instructors encourage adherence to fitness programs is by encouraging social supports among participants. This is especially helpful if the participants in the fitness class know one another. A fitness instructor can encourage each participant to call those participants that he or she knows to make sure that they will be attending class. The participants in the class can also get together to discuss their fitness goals and the state of the class in general. Many beginning participants would benefit by having an experienced mentor within the class. This mentor would be responsible for making sure the new participant attends all the classes and keeps efficient documentation of progress. In order to encourage the social supports, the fitness instructor could suggest that participants invite their friends and family to join the exercise class.

Developing group camaraderie -- One of the most important things a fitness instructor can do is encourage camaraderie among the participants. If the participants in the fitness class make strong social contexts with one another, they will be more likely to adhere to the fitness program. A good way to initiate this process is to have the members of the class introduce themselves to one another at the beginning of the fitness program. During the warm-up and cool-down portions of the class, the instructor may encourage the students to talk amongst themselves. The instructor should not allow any members of the class to diminish morale by complaining or criticizing other participants.

Emphasizing the positive -- A physical fitness instructor should always take care to emphasize the positive aspects of the participants' performance. Many individuals will begin in an exercise class with trepidation and self-doubt. It is the job of a fitness instructor to allay these concerns, and demonstrably show to all the participants that progress can be made if honest effort is given. It is inevitable that some aspects of the fitness program will be less enjoyable than others; a fitness instructor should take care to emphasize the positive consequences of seemingly difficult work. The fitness instructor should take care to remind the participants of the long-term fitness goals, so as to ensure that participants maintain the high level of effort.

Preparing participants for changes -- Over the course of a long fitness program, it is inevitable that there will be some interruptions. In order to minimize the damage done by these interruptions, the fitness instructor should take care to warn participants. For instance, if a fitness instructor is aware that he or she will have to miss one or more classes, then he or she should introduce the substitute instructor to the class at the earliest convenience. If the instructor knows that he or she will have to be absent for a long period of time, it is especially important to cultivate self-monitoring skills in the participants. Also, it is important for the instructor to notify participants of any significant changes in the structure or contents of the exercise class. In the event the class must be canceled for some unforeseen reason, it is a good idea for participants to have a basic routine that they can perform individually.

Emphasizing healthy lifestyles -- In order for the participants in an exercise class to reach their fitness goals, they need to maintain a healthy lifestyle outside of the class environment. A well-trained fitness instructor will be informed on the issues of nutrition and weight control, and will be able to provide specific guidelines to the participants in the class. It may be helpful for the instructor to provide lists of appropriate foods for the participants in the class, as well as to provide forms on which participants can document their food and drink consumption. The achievement of long-term goals in the fitness class should be based not only on physical performance within the class environment, but on adherence to nutritional requirements outside of class.

Rejecting defeatism -- Many of the participants in an exercise class will begin with a self-conscious and insecure mindset. It is important for the fitness instructor to not let this attitude deteriorate into defeatism. Temporary setbacks in the fitness class should not be allowed to degenerate into long term problems. In order to minimize defeatism in the fitness class, the instructor should always accentuate the positive aspects of performance. Even those participants who are struggling the most with the requirements of the exercise class should be given regular positive feedback.

Continuing Exercise

Studies have shown that a large proportion of individuals who begin exercise programs drop out at least to some extent within short periods of time. Many of those who discontinue their protocols can be easily identified upfront by verbal questioning or completion of questionnaires. Ways to increase their daily physical activities should be identified in addition to a prescribed exercise program because this increases participation and adherence. Trials have been performed that indicate that such lifestyle changes can be equally as effective as formal programs in terms of fitness, symptoms, and improvement in anthropometric measurements.

USDA Dietary Guidelines

The United States Department of Agriculture began issuing nutrition guidelines in 1894, and in 1943 the department began promoting the Basic 7 food groups. In 1956, Basic 7 was replaced with the Basic Four food groups. These were fruits and vegetables, cereals and breads, milk, and meat. Basic Four lasted until 1992, when it was replaced with the Food Pyramid, which divided food into six groups: 1) Bread, cereal, rice, pasta 2) Fruit 3) Vegetables 4) Meat, poultry, fish, dry beans, eggs, nuts 5) Milk, yogurt, cheese 6) Fats, oils, sweets. The Food Pyramid also provided recommendations for the number of daily servings from each group.

Exercise Training

Muscular Fitness

Muscular fitness is characterized by the range of motion for optimal movement and several components of muscular strength. Range of motion around a joint area takes into account the properties of any tissue attached there, not just muscles. Muscular strength includes the highest force that can be exerted during one contraction and the ability to maintain continual contractions without tiring. Strength is usually approximated as the amount of weight that the person can lift. If this force is multiplied by the distance traveled through, actual work performed results. Most measurements of strength can be done in most training settings with current equipment, but endurance can also be evaluated using the person's own body weight in some way. A composite measurement is force or power where the ability to perform sudden, dramatic movements is evaluated according to the length moved relative to time involved; power is defined as the amount of work done in a particular time period.

Physiologically, one of the most important features of muscular strength is neurological programming, which contributes by increasing the effectiveness of contraction patterns that have been previously learned. If muscles have been repeatedly utilized, such as during an exercise program, the dimensions and sometimes the number of the muscle fibers and other muscle components expand allowing greater strength. Complex endocrine changes, particularly involving increased protein production, can occur with weight training and therefore augment strength. The category of fiber influences muscular force with the faster-twitch types providing more one repetition strength. Muscle mass is an important concept as well, especially in the case of sedentary, frail, or elderly individuals, where they have lost a lot of this mass and concomitant muscular strength.

Maximal Isotonic Strength

As currently evaluated, the term isotonic strength is incorrectly used. In theory, "isotonic" means a consistent force or tension working against another outside workload. In reality, this never really occurs even while measuring during resistance training because the workload needs to be displaced from its position and then moved to the desired location. The one repetition maximum (1RM) is ideally the test to measure this so-called isotonic strength because it represents the greatest resistance that can be lifted or lowered. These heavy loads should be moved to position slowly, taking up to 5 seconds. Sometimes, more repetitions are done with less than peak workloads and the 1RM extrapolated.

Isotonic muscular endurance tests really measure a mixture of isotonic strength coupled with the ability to overcome the initial inertia to move the resistance. The idea here is to see how many repetitions at less than peak workloads an individual can perform before they tire. Free weights, machines, or the subject's own body weight can be used as the resistance. Usually, a one repetition maximum has been previously determined, and a particular percentage of that is selected and the number of repetitions before fatigue is quantified. Fit subjects can do more repetitions at a particular percentage of their 1RM. Their endurance has been improved when they can perform more repetitions.

In pure isometric exercises, muscles are not allowed to contract because both ends are fixed in some way. During evaluations of muscular strength, endurance, and power, modifications of isometric exercises can be employed. A parameter called the maximal voluntary isometric contraction is often used to evaluate peak isometric strength. In this case, the maximum contraction that can be performed against a fixed resistance like a hand grip is measured. Endurance is trickier to measure because in this case what is being quantified is the rate of deterioration of the strength required to maintain the isometric exercise. In order to evaluate isometric power, sophisticated equipment is usually required in order to generate a plot of time versus force and measure the area and slopes until a maximal contraction is achieved.

Isokinetic Dynamometer

An isokinetic dynamometer is a device that allows the individual being evaluated to use different types of contractions in a controlled manner at a consistent speed. The machine moves different parts while the person applies resistance against that part and then computerized evaluations are done. The types of possible movements and evaluations are numerous. In particular, isokinetic strength, the ability to shorten or lengthen the muscle at an invariable rate, can be quantified. In addition, endurance can be evaluated under similar conditions by performing many repetitions, averaging the force the individual is able to supply during the first few beginning reps versus the end of the testing, and looking at the ratio between these measurements. This device also incorporates a protractor that can measure range of motion around a joint.

Free Weights vs. Weight Machines

Many experts feel that using free weights in exercise programs is superior to using weight machines primarily because using free weights approximates daily joint and muscle usage better than machines. A larger number of muscle groups and joints are usually activated during use of free weights which means a higher workload can theoretically be achieved. The drawbacks to use of free weights center on the learning curve for usage and perceived safety issues (which have not really been documented). On the other hand, the main arguments for use of weight machines are that they are generally not dangerous or difficult to use even for beginners and that they each work on the fitness of a particular desired muscle group. However, the main disadvantages are the restrictions these machines place on the pattern and amount of movement and the lack of portability.

Contraindications

The typical conditions precluding exercise testing are comprised of unstable, uncontrolled or new changes reflecting cardiac or pulmonary conditions. Presence of a current systemic infection would contraindicate testing as well. Examples of cardiac-related contraindications include uncontrollable chest pain, arrhythmias, and heart failure. Presence of pulmonary blood clots is another reason to avoid testing. The health care provider may upon complete consideration of some other indications decide whether to do exercise testing. Some examples of these considerations would be extreme hypertension, electrolyte imbalances, certain cardiac problems, presence of other disorders that can be provoked when exercising, persistent infectious diseases such as AIDS, unmanageable metabolic disorders like diabetes, or some other physical or mental disability.

Range of Motion

Range of motion, sometimes called flexibility, around a specific joint structure is governed by a number of directly connected internal parameters as well to a lesser extent the outside or peripheral environment. Different types of joints operate differently in terms of the freedom of movement dictated by their structure and the arrangement of the connecting bones. The suppleness or ability to stretch muscles and other connecting tissues contributes greatly to range of motion, and these are parameters that can be improved by doing stretching exercises. The way in which the neuromuscular system responds to movement around a joint can significantly influence the range of motion because there are two different mechanisms that can be activated during stretching. Initially structures called muscle spindles activate sensory messages that ultimately cause the muscle to become taut, but if the stretch is held longer either inhibitory signals or nerve endings called golgi tendon organs (GTO) are summoned and cause the muscle to loosen up and become more flexible. Heat at the joint area or externally increases flexibility as well.

Range of motion or flexibility can be improved by exercises that are either dynamic or static in nature, meaning that the joint either responds to the connecting musculature or is just moved by someone else. The most commonly utilized static stretches are done by alternating stretching and contracting portions against the resistance of another individual. Yoga is primarily static in nature as well. Most other stretching exercises are dynamic. They include maintaining a stretch near the limits of range of motion, using gravity to enhance the stretch, programming the muscles and nerves by doing a measured and prolonged stretch for at least 30 seconds, or bouncing another body part against the joint to stretch it. This latter type of ballistic stretching may cause injury, however. Range of motion quickly deteriorates if stretching is not done regularly. Stretching should be performed daily if possible, including 2 to 4 reps each of a variety of targeted exercises.

Often flexibility is approximated by observing the response to a variety of field tests emphasizing stretching. Some of the most common tests evaluate the range of motion in the hip, leg and shoulder regions. For example, typical exercises to assess flexibility in the hip region might address the ability to rotate the thigh while seated or stretch the leg above while prone. The angle that the leg can be pulled up toward the back or stretched forward with a flat foot might be measured. The angle that the arms can stretch backwards or touch the other appendage from behind might be calculated. Typically, the difference in response on the right or left side of the body is recorded. The goal of exercise programs involving stretching is to increase these angles; in other words, the range of motion is augmented.

MUSCLE CHANGES

Current theories claim that there are is actually a continuous, seamless series of muscle fiber types defined by the differences in two proteins, myosin ATPase and myosin heavy chain. When resistance training is incorporated into an exercise program, changes in these proteins can occur and a particular muscle fiber can change its type. This phenomenon along with sensory adaptations can increase strength. In addition, studies suggest that with resistance exercise programs the relative geometry between muscle fibers is changed. In particular, the numbers of muscles that are pulling at an angle appear to be increased, which is one effect of this training that may be detrimental.

STRENGTH TRAINING

Isometric type exercises in which there is limited contraction against an immovable force such as a hand grip are really only appropriate during the initial period of rehabilitation when range of motion might be minimal. They are probably contraindicated for cardiac patients because these types of exercises tend to increase blood pressure. Isotonic type exercises utilizing free weights provide relatively constant changes through a range of motion and are advantageous for many types of individuals as long as all phases and ROM are incorporated and the program is adapted to the person's goals. Isokinetic training is typically performed in a medical treatment or athletic training setting because it involves use of complex machinery and interpretation, but the controlled environment it provides makes it very useful for increasing strength parameters.

MUSCLE SORENESS

If muscles become sore while an individual is exercising or shortly thereafter, metabolic waste has probably accumulated in the area and augmented sensory pain responses. These effects are usually transitory. On the other hand, many people experience muscle tenderness a day or two after they exercise. In this case, current hypotheses as to the causes of this pain suggest that some sort of damage has occurred to the muscle during the lengthening phase of the exercise. This damage upsets the regulation of the contraction-relaxation response by Ca^{2+}, triggers inflammatory pathways, and liberates highly reactive molecules that can augment muscle destruction. Eventually other stabilizing proteins are formed to mend the damage and soreness disappears.

THE VALSALVA MANEUVER

The Valsalva maneuver is a breathing event that often occurs during intense resistance type exercise. Basically, what occurs is that the individual attempts to exhale intensely but the voice box area is shut. As a consequence, pressure is increased inside the chest. This results in very high blood pressure as well. Therefore, proper breathing technique needs to be taught to individuals doing resistance exercises. They need to be taught to breathe in during the lengthening portion each procedure and then breathe out during the shortening portion. In this way, they can avoid the Valsalva maneuver during exhalation.

Proper Technique

In addition to proper breathing technique, there are other ways to insure a safe environment. When using some type of free weight or barbell, the individual needs to know how to stand or lie correctly to maintain balance. This basically involves having all their weight aligned under the shoulders in the upright position or the major parts of the body connected to the floor or support if lying down throughout the exercise. The person should stand with flat feet and flexed knees. The person should use a weight that can be fully gripped with the hand completely encircling it. If they chose to use some type of weight belt, which can provide stability, they need to watch the speed at which they do the exercise and possibly monitor blood pressure because the portion on diastole may be heightened. An added safety precaution that the exercise professional or helper may provide is to watch the person during the exercise and be there to help them complete any part they are having difficulty with.

Resistance-Type Exercise Program

When an exercise professional is designing a resistance-type program for an individual, they first need to plan exercises that are specific to the individual's goals, state of health, and range of motion. It is useful to include exercises that cover all major muscle groups, but with these principles in mind. Exercises need to be varied in order to avoid stagnant cycles where no improvement is shown or the muscle group is excessively taxed. One way to achieve this variation is to incorporate shorter cycles of shifting emphasis (for example, strength, power, or endurance) within the much longer time frame of the total exercise plan. Lastly, over time the complexity of the exercise and the workload should be progressively increased.

Resistance-type exercises that target sets of core muscles should always be performed first. In this case, core muscular groups are all of the bigger ones like the upper torso or the back that involve a number of joints. If strengthening the core muscles is the goal, some exercises that are aimed at muscles around one joint such as those found in the extremities should still be done afterwards. Areas targeted by these assistance-type exercises should be rotated. If the major goal is to enhance muscle groups in the extremities, the larger muscle groups should still be addressed first and then exercises should switch back and forth between muscles that balance out each other in the arms and legs. In the case of very specific programs, the sequence is still large groups first and then high followed by lower workload joint-specific exercises.

Generally, resistance training should not be done every day of the week because the muscles need to bounce back between sessions. This means that initially resistance training should only be prescribed up to 3 days a week. As the program progresses, a day or more may be added but specific muscle groups are never exercised more than 3 days a week. The workload is a tricky variable to prescribe. Most recommendations are to do 8 to 12 repetitions to fatigue but there are many variations. A general guideline is that if an individual can exceed the specified number of reps by at least two over a couple of successive sessions, they are probably ready to incorporate an incrementally larger workload the next time. A percentage of the one repetition maximum is usually targeted as well with the percentage increasing with training level. The individual's goals play a role here too. If the major purpose is to augment strength the emphasis is on increasing the weight, if the goal is more endurance then the number of repetitions are generally increased, and if more power is desired some very fast but lower intensity exercises are included.

The total amount of training performed in one session is the product all the repetitions and the computation of all the resistances utilized. As an individual progresses toward the fitness level of a genuine athlete, sometimes this training volume can be increased by using heavier weights or more than one series of repetitions. Increasing the total amount of training dramatically during a single session is generally not recommended however. The amount of time a person rests between exercises should be dictated by the type of exercise they are performing and their goals. In general, the duration of rest between different exercises is less if the goal is to improve endurance. Otherwise, rebounding from exercises that involve the large muscle groups can take up to 3 minutes, while those that involve single joints require only a minute or two. Most studies suggest that only very fit and trained individuals should include exercises that are very fast or jerky.

Spinal Cord Injuries

Classifications of spinal cord injuries primarily relate to either the area that was damaged or the extent of the impairment. The vast majority of these injuries result from some sort of external traumatic event, although somatic diseases can be responsible. The degree of loss of muscular and/or neurological function is directly related to the area of the spinal cord that was damaged. In other words, if the area afflicted is higher in the cord, more impairment is seen. Thus, some classifications pinpoint the exact nerves damaged with those in the neck region controlling upper extremities and upper torso, those in the upper back affecting the chest and abdomen, those in the lower back controlling lower extremities, and the ones near the base relating to excretion and sexual function. More commonly, people with spinal cord injuries are identified by the extent of their injury. Any impairment to the nerves in the cervical region will weaken neuromuscular responses in all extremities and the torso and is usually referred to as tetraplegia. Damage lower than that usually renders the individual paraplegic, which means the lower limbs and possibly the torso are affected. The relative loss of motor or sensory function is sometimes used to stratify patients as well.

Spinal cord injury (SPI) patients have normal neurological functions for anything controlled above the level of injury. They will not be able to perform functions controlled at or below the point of injury, and will experience involuntary muscle contractions in the lower areas. Therefore, individuals with SPI typically cannot control their bladder and bowel, and if they are tetraplegic the nerves and subsequent muscle groups leading to vital functions in the upper body such as cardiac and glandular systems are affected as well. These patients are prone to bone breakage because of loss of minerals to the bones. They are susceptible to bladder infections, upper extremity overuse problems, joint damage and loss of ROM, and pulmonary infections if the upper body is affected.

Spinal cord injury patients usually need to be connected to some sort of electrical induction device in order to perform exercise. This is because on their own they really cannot move their bigger muscle groups. In addition, they cannot signal their ancillary systems that in a normal individual would be involved in blood flow and oxygen uptake changes during exercise. For these reasons, cardiovascular parameters need to be monitored in these patients because their involuntary reflexes can be manifested all at once and they may become extremely hypertensive setting off a variety of associated symptoms like low heart rate and profuse sweating.

Exercise tests for spinal cord injury patients are always some version of arm cycle ergometry with subsequent approximation of maximal oxygen uptake. There are a number of field tests for which equations have been developed to predict this peak uptake from cranking at lesser loads as well as other procedures that incrementally increase the workload in a laboratory setting to form similar approximations. There is also a protocol that determines peak oxygen usage by measuring the furthest distance the individual can race their wheelchair in a given time period. For all these tests, the room must be relatively cool, the individual's body must be securely and comfortably fastened to the equipment, the person should expel their urine before the test, and they should wear constrictive clothing that keeps their blood pressure in line. The usual parameters should be monitored during and particularly after the test because these people tend to develop low blood pressure and exhaustion.

Most studies suggest that if possible both arm and leg ergometry should be included in an exercise program for SCI patients. Exercise design for paraplegic SCI individuals targets the upper body and typically includes arm-crank ergometry or specialized wheelchair ergometry in which the same type of chair that they normally use is attached to some other type of equipment. Hemodynamic and pulmonary values have shown improvement with this type of program. Because of some loss of muscle use, it is important to monitor cardiovascular and gas exchange parameters that may be impaired. Arm cycle ergometry is prescribed for some tetraplegic SCI patients but because of their more limited muscle use, it may be of limited value. Use of attached hydraulic machinery did enhance strength and aerobic values in one study group. Usually electrical stimulation is required and they may need to perform these exercises lying down. For the most part, improvements in strength and oxygen uptake appear to involve only local muscle groups. For some, aquatic exercises, wheelchair-based sports, flexibility improvement, and limited aerobics are appropriate.

Spina Bifida

Spina bifida (SB) is a spinal deformity present at birth which is usually immediately corrected with surgery. Nevertheless, the underlying causes of SB are related to spinal cord damage, with the vast majority of these patients having damage in the lower lumbosacral region. This area controls the excretory and sexual organs so they are usually prone to urinary tract infections. One of the major problems in most of these individuals is that cerebrospinal fluid cannot be properly controlled and thus builds up in the brain unless it is mechanically diverted elsewhere (usually somewhere in the torso). Other neurological issues requiring intervention range from pressure in the brain to fluid retention in or elongation of the spinal cord itself. With age, these individuals also often develop distortions of the back and other areas, upper body problems, bone loss, painful skin areas, and weight problems.

If they can walk, spina bifida patients appear to benefit from treadmill walking or use of a cycle; the functional responses increase most if the impairment is relatively low in the lumbosacral region. Some studies have suggested that use of arm cycles or upper body free weights may augment some parameters. If the SB patient uses a wheelchair, they can perform these types of exercises as well as cycle ergometry using their legs. Many spina bifida patients experience some loss of voluntary movement in their lower limbs so electrical stimulation of these areas will not work.

Therefore, it is difficult to incorporate lower body movements for these individuals. Any type of equipment containing latex should be avoided because the majority of SB patients have a unique allergic response to it.

Multiple Sclerosis

Multiple sclerosis (MS) is a neuromuscular disorder affecting the central nervous system. It is autoimmune in nature and appears to be exacerbated by a number of factors, in particular infections. Normally fatty and protein-containing substances cover and protect nerve endings, but in MS these substances are stripped off and accumulate elsewhere. Immunological responses to these substances, in particular two types of these myelin proteins, set off a cascade of inflammatory events. Injury occurs in the inflamed regions of the brain and spinal cord. As a result, neurological abnormalities associated with these regions develop over time and result in a diagnosis of multiple sclerosis. Episodes of MS are usually transitory but persistent. Typical symptoms are blurred or temporarily absent vision unilaterally, lack of sensations such as taste, inability to synchronize movements, loss of excretory control, sexual problems, absence of feeling in the lower body, and memory problems.

If cardio and respiratory parameters are measured in a multiple sclerosis patient during exercise, they tend to correlate well with workload just as in a healthy individual. Most of the time, however, they cannot reach the maximal oxygen uptake levels of their age-matched normal group, probably because they tend to become fatigued and stop or exercise below capacity. If the individual is affected by spasms, they do not have much muscle strength either, but if they are not spastic, they may be able to perform these exercises better. Because these patients experience many sensory defects and are often sedentary, muscle groups can waste away and become very weak. Therefore, they rarely perform strength exercises near theoretical levels. Nevertheless, limited studies on exercise programs in MS patients suggest that they can augment their muscular power and endurance. Typical programs incorporate resistance training, stretching, and oxygen-consuming activities, often water aerobics.

A patient with multiple sclerosis can usually undergo the normal type of exercise test components for muscular strength and aerobic capacity as long as appropriate safety precautions are taken. For example, they may not have much range of motion at or below the hip area and their equilibrium is often impacted. Tests to evaluate these parameters should be performed first. In addition, the mode of endurance testing is often dictated by muscular defects in the foot or ankle area. Commonly, the muscles in the region where the toes flex are weakened so that these patients should be tested on a cycle. If fragility extends to the ankle area, then they need to be fastened to the machine. Incremental increases in workload are usually added to a less than theoretically peak target.

Stroke

A stroke is actually a neuromuscular event that occurs in the brain. The genesis of stroke is either interrupted vascular blood flow to the brain as a result of clotting or other obstructions (in close to 90% of cases) or a hemorrhage occurring within the main part of the brain, the cerebrum, or the middle subarachnoid portion. The latter causes massive internal bleeding in the brain. As a result, neurological ability is impaired. Because the precipitating event in a stroke is clearly cardiovascular in nature, treatment or prevention is similar, like lowering risk factors, pharmacological control with aspirin and anti-hypertensive drugs, or surgery to clear or keep open the blood vessels, in particular the carotid artery.

Exercise testing and prescription in a patient who has had a stroke is dictated by their neuromuscular defects and probable underlying cardiovascular problems. These individuals usually have impaired balance and walking patterns, which makes use of a fixed cycle ergometer the best way to perform aerobic fitness testing. If they are very weak or paralyzed in some way, an arm cycle might be used despite its greater cardiovascular workload. Incremental power increases until exhaustion may be used if parameters such as blood pressure are monitored. Standard protocols to measure strength and range of motion are used with the caveat that abilities on either side of the body may vary greatly and need to be quantified.

The type and total amount of training that a stroke survivor can participate in is extremely dependent on the quantity of muscle mass that remains operative. Those patients who are paralyzed or very weak may only be able to do exercises that remove or lessen gravitational forces such as maintaining a position the exercise professional has preset or lifting a limb without the additional use of weights.

Emphasis should be put on using equipment and exercises that increase core stability like resistance bands. The cardiovascular portion of the exercise program should be done in a supervised environment for at least 60 minutes a day, three days a week, and can be done on a variety of equipment. The main restrictions are to maintain a heart rate determined by the prior exercise test and to select exercises that accommodate their possible cardiovascular, balance and gait problems. Range of motion drills should accentuate stretching the musculature of the stroke victim's weak side. Blood pressure and heart rate should be constantly monitored.

Traumatic Brain Injury

When an individual encounters a blow to the head, they undergo a sequence of events known as traumatic brain injury (TBI). Sometimes this damage is minimal involving very short-term loss of awareness or other mental capacity and localized neurological problems. Often, however, the effects are much more devastating and long-lasting. Typically, when the blow is sustained, there is not only brain injury where the impact struck but also an instantaneous ricochet effect in other parts of the brain. Nerves and blood vessels in the area are damaged and blood leaches into the brain causing it to swell and possibly protrude into the area of the spine. Parts of the nerve cells can eventually begin to die and the cranial cavity then actually shrinks in size. When the brain is deprived of oxygen, similar effects can occur.

Initially, the severity of traumatic brain injury is usually assessed in terms of the person's degree of awareness relative to a complete coma with emphasis on their neuromotor reactions. The scope of the brain injury is usually evaluated by magnetic resonance imaging or computerized tomography. Specific neurological defects, in isolation or tandem, should eventually be noted as they can help localize the areas of brain damage and aid in the development of a treatment plan. Specific behavioral patterns tend to originate from particular portions of the brain, and specific nerves have been found to control different acuities as well. For TBI the injured nerve can sometimes be pinpointed whereas oxygen deprivation tends to cause more systemic effects. Some TBI patients develop transitory high blood pressure, or later seizures or tissue deposition of Ca^{2+}.

TBI patients are usually either quite young people, with motor vehicle accidents as the primary cause, or very elderly individuals who have fallen. Therefore, there can be a wide range of fitness levels represented in the group. In a clinical setting, exercise testing for aerobic capacity might involve use of a treadmill or ergometer with the individual's weight at least somewhat supported or stabilized with straps or a sling. If these are unavailable, a walking test with progressively increasing speed is sometimes used. Evaluations of motor functions should be included. Muscle parameters are very important due to expected weakness and limited range of motion. When designing an exercise program for a TBI patient, the most common prescription is some variation of walking. The prevalence of balance problems in these individuals might dictate other aerobic activities as well as stabilizing modifications to resistance training. Since these patients have difficulty self-measuring their heart rate, either monitors or their perceptions are usually used to determine workloads.

Parkinson's Disease

There are actually three different classifications of Parkinson's Disease (PD), all of which involve the gradual deterioration of neurological functions and subsequent loss of motor skills. In two of the types, secondary and multi-system, causative agents have been recognized, but the etiology for the vast majority of PD is unknown and thus termed idiopathic. This latter version manifests itself in one of three ways, depending on the most prevalent clinical indications. Some people with PD of unknown origin primarily tremble but do not experience other significant neurological problems. Others have more serious problems with their alignment and walking patterns, and another group is very stiff and can hardly move. Many individuals with Parkinson's Disease cannot control their involuntary functions.

There are actually no conclusive procedures used to diagnose Parkinson's Disease. Usually the behavioral pattern of the individual is observed during physical examination or subsequent exercise testing. There are a number of simple tests that the clinician can perform to look for presence of tremor upon stress, gait and balance issues, or deterioration of movement. The individual should also be evaluated for levels of other neuromuscular abilities such as processing thoughts and performing other muscular tasks. Exercise professionals should watch the walking patterns of the PD patient to determine the best modes for exercise. Muscular power often needs to be evaluated using assistive devices. Most parkinsonism is treated with drugs that either deplete high levels of acetylcholine or enhance levels of dopamine, which transmits nerve impulses to the brain. Occasionally brain surgery or manipulation is performed. Exercise programs should be individualized and take into account all PD and other issues.

Cerebral Palsy

Cerebral palsy (CP) is a disorder where the brain has been damaged early in life resulting in neuromotor functional abnormalities that do not get progressively worse. CP occurs most often in children who were born pre-term or whose weight was significantly below normal. A variety of causes have been suggested, including infectious agents and traumatic events. The disorder is characterized by spastic movements that the child cannot control, abnormally high or low muscle tone, greater acuity on one side of the body with resultant posture problems, and an increased incidence of curvature of the spine. Symptoms often go unrecognized until the child is several years old. Treatments usually involve surgery to either alleviate the muscle spasms by rearrangement of tendons or bones, or to rectify the spinal abnormalities.

When performing exercise testing in a cerebral palsy patient, the aerobic endurance section often consists of progressively small increases in workload using an arm cycle. If the person exhibits some functionality in their lower limbs, a step machine variant in which the individual is lying back while pedaling with all 4 limbs is a good choice. Occasionally, testing might be done on a treadmill if the CP patient can walk but safety issues are a concern. Muscular assessments are appropriate as long as accommodations for impaired balance and relative lack of core strength are made. When prescribing an exercise program for these CP patients, use of aerobic machines should be done at very low levels, stretching should be incorporated and performed in stable positions, and machines that can regulate the speed and range of motion should be emphasized. The paramount considerations are depression of spastic activity and maintenance of balance.

Postpolio Syndrome

Postpolio syndrome (PPS) is the term for the delayed reemergence of symptoms related to prior infection with the polio virus. The polio virus and resultant disease called poliomyelitis have largely been eliminated and were most prevalent a half century ago. Polio is a neuromuscular disease in which the virus damages nerves in the lower extremities and the associated muscle groups become weak and shrunken and possibly paralyzed. Usually after a few months, some of the nerve endings start to regenerate and neuromuscular function is restored. However, many years later this dynamic process may reach a point where nerve damage exceeds regeneration, and then symptoms reappear resulting in PPS. Diagnosis of this syndrome is done primarily by doing tests to rule out other neuromuscular diseases or other issues involving pain in the lower extremities, although wasting muscle groups in this area are good indications of the condition. Other possible diagnostic tools include continued presence of the polio virus, electromyography, and patient history.

PPS is primarily treated symptomatically. Nonsteroidal anti-inflammatory drugs and pharmacologic agents that loosen up the muscles are the most common types of symptomatic relief. These patients may also be receiving treatment for depression. In order to make walking more comfortable, these individuals are often fitted for a variety of braces and shoe lifts. Typical exercise testing consists of endurance testing utilizing dual type ergometers engaging both arms and legs and more functional types of testing for muscular parameters such as recording the time and form for tasks like multi-parameter walking sequences. PPS is classified basically according to current and previous history of symptoms. Exercise programs are encouraged for all classifications except in the patient who is symptomatic including evidence of current muscular and neurological degeneration. Otherwise, the intensity, number of metabolic equivalents, length of session and number of days per week exercise is performed are dictated by the severity and evidence of recent symptoms. Typical modes of exercise are dual type ergometers and swimming.

Guillain-Barre Syndrome

Guillain-Barre syndrome (GBS) is an autoimmune disease directed against a portion of the myelin in the nerves in the extremities. Thus, the effects are neuromuscular and include muscular weakness and possible loss of movement that tends to travel up the body in the acute phase. The causative agents appear to be infectious, neoplastic, or pharmacologic in nature. Most GBS patients eventually show improvement; symptoms recede primarily to the lower extremities and may become relatively negligible over time for some people. Drugs to treat depression, muscle spasms, or discomfort are often administered. Mild rehabilitation programs are often instituted clinically in the acute phase, as well as later. Unfortunately, studies relating to exercise testing and programs for these individuals are sparse, but there is some suggestion of their utility. If performed, these tests and drills should be down in positions that help maintain the person's balance such as seated or lying down.

Myopathies

Any muscle disease that is characterized by muscle weakness and wasting and is either inherited or developed is encompassed in the umbrella term "myopathy". The most common type of inherited myopathy is some variant of muscular dystrophy in which the predominant weak region is in the core muscles which may extend to cardiac muscle involvement. Another common congenital variant involves weakness in the muscles of the face. Myopathies that are acquired are typically metabolic, immunologic (including infectious), or pharmacologic in origin. Differential diagnostic procedures include a range of chemical, immunological, metabolic, stimulatory, and scanning tests as well as examination of a portion of the muscle microscopically. The most common intervention for all these types is corticosteroid use coupled with flexibility exercises. Occasionally, surgery to lengthen the tendons is indicated.

Any patient presenting with a myopathy should be evaluated for muscle strength. One test that is sort of unique to this group of patients measures lactic acid and ammonia prior to and after forearm exercises performed with the use of a blood pressure cuff; the purpose is to identify one type called glycogen storage disease. Exercise programs depend to an extent on the type of disorder. If the patient has muscular dystrophy or some other type of inherited problem, cardiac muscle should first be evaluated by ultrasound after stress. Emphasis is on high rep low workload programs that progress over time. Other types of myopathies may require very specific environments or nutritional supplements. For example, there are several disorders that are render the individual sensitive to temperature, and several of the metabolic variants dictate careful timing of carbohydrate consumption. The value of strength training and exercises to improve ventilatory muscles in these patients has not been unequivocally shown.

Peripheral Neuropathy

An impairment of the architecture or functionality of a nerve cell (or its components) that occurs without CNS involvement is termed peripheral neuropathy. Intense acute focused pain may or may not be associated with this disorder. Peripheral neuropathy can be caused by a variety of infectious agents, the spread of tumor cells, traumatic events, metabolic diseases, and more. The actual presentation of the disorder can vary by number of nerves affected and distribution of dysfunction. Therefore, identification of the affected areas by a series of neurological and reflex tests is very important. Additional laboratory tests to pinpoint the cause are usually done as well such as magnetic resonance imaging to find tumors or other tissue abnormalities, identification of the involved nerves through use of electrical techniques or anesthesia, or blood tests to look for immunological or metabolic abnormalities.

Pharmacologic treatment of peripheral neuropathy is really related to pain relief. If the pain is not severe, over-the-counter drugs like aspirin may suffice. Typically, however, most individuals with neuropathic pain also take drugs usually prescribed for depression or convulsions. If their pain presents suddenly or is very piercing, the convulsions need to be controlled first. Opium-containing drugs have also been used but not as effectively. Pain management can also be aided by use of orthotic devices, temporary nerve blockage, selective nerve-triggering techniques, relaxation, and elimination if possible, of the root cause of the disorder. Well-designed rehabilitation programs play a vital role.

Physician approval should be obtained before doing exercise testing or designing a program for patients with peripheral neuropathy. This is because the design is really dependent on identification of the underlying cause of the disorder and its possible elimination as well as other health and mental issues. When performing exercise testing, the professional should concentrate on measurement of muscular strength and ROM. It is important to note what exacerbates the pain. Exercise programs are usually designed to rehabilitate the individual in terms muscular parameters and range of motion in the affected region. Initially, only external stimulation or manipulation might be appropriate, but eventually exercises directly involving the patient should be incorporated. Traditional components of programs for these individuals have centered on enjoyable aerobic activities like dancing or walking that they do several times a week as well as core strength and flexibility drills.

Neoplasm

A neoplasm is an abnormal growth of tissue somewhere in the body. Sometimes these growths are confined to a particular area and cannot spread. However, other growths contain cells whose genetic structure has changed and regulation of cell growth has been lost. These latter cancerous cells have the potential to attack other cells in the region of the growth as well as distally. Malignancies are normally classified according to the type of cell and area from which they develop. Development and progression of each type of cancer is for the most part malignancy-specific. There is some suggestion of genetic predisposition to certain cancers but the most important risk factors appear to be smoking, inadequate nutrition, and sedentary lifestyle with excess weight.

Cancer

There are now a number of screening tests for common cancers which can be used as adjuncts to tissue biopsy and pathological examination in order to provide a diagnosis of cancer. Lung cancer is actually the most common cancer in terms of mortality, in part due to the absence of any adequate test to screen for it. Otherwise, the most prevalent cancer in men is prostate carcinoma, with a very good laboratory test called prostate-specific antigen to detect it. For women, breast carcinoma is the most widespread, which can be detected by a number of means with the gold standard being a mammogram. Colorectal carcinoma can be detected by a number of procedures, most authoritatively by colonoscopy, which inserts a tube into the area. All of these cancers have symptomatic warning signs including among other things breast lumps, evidence of blood in stools or sputum, and difficulty urinating for breast, colorectal, lung, and prostate carcinomas respectively. All of these particular cancer types originate from surface layer cells on the respective organs. They are staged according to the measurements of the tumor itself, as well as whether lymph nodes in the immediate area or more distal sites have been infiltrated with these uncontrolled cells.

Surgical intervention in some form is most often done to remove some or all of the cancerous cells. Sometimes only a small amount of tissue is excised in the area and in these cases other modalities must be used as adjuncts. One of these adjuncts is bombardment of the cancerous area with radiation in order to selectively destroy the abnormal deoxyribonucleic acid and prevent further malignant cell growth. Another treatment mode is use of chemotherapeutic drugs which target cancerous cell death relative to normal cells. If the tumor growth is stimulated by hormones, antagonistic agents that inhibit these hormones are useful. Cells from cancers of the immune system may be killed by corticosteroids. All of these chemotherapeutic and systemic agents have associated side effects. More extensive surgical interventions are still performed today. Here larger areas are excised, adjoining lymph nodes are usually drained, and agents listed above may be utilized as well.

Most systemic adjunctive therapeutic agents for cancer are administered either intravenously or orally. Most of these treatments would be termed chemotherapeutic agents; in other words, they are some type of drug. Many of these are antimetabolites, like methotrexate or fluorouracil. Other modes of action include alkylating agents that prevent DNA recoil and cell reproduction such as cyclophosphamide or incorporation of platinum salts such as cisplatin. Side effects are plentiful blood cell abnormalities, extreme tiredness, and nausea. Often bone transplantation is done in the same time frame. Hormonal agents may be taken orally to treat hormone-dependent tumors, including, for example, the antiestrogen tamoxifen.

No definitive studies have established that exercise can cure or combat cancer, but it does provide psychosocial and physiological benefits. Any patient diagnosed early or one who has survived cancer (generally thought of as 5 years post diagnosis) can perform general exercise testing as long as they do not have comorbidities. Other patients can perform modifications. The area of excision, presence of associated symptoms, and blood cell parameters dictate the actual types of tests to be done or avoid. Attempts should be made to duplicate as closely as possible the subsequent exercise program. The most commonly prescribed exercise for individuals with or surviving cancer is walking because it uses many large muscle groups without jarring, but sometimes cycling is preferred. In general, they should exercise at least 3 days a week for a minimum of 20 minutes but sometimes several shorter periods can be interspersed with resting. One important consideration is that if the patient is currently taking chemotherapeutic drugs, their immune system is suppressed and thus they cannot exercise for longer uninterrupted periods.

Immune System

Any material that the body perceives as foreign elicits a response in the immune system. Viruses, bacteria, and fungi are all viewed as foreign or antigenic. If they penetrate the first lines of defense such as the skin or mucosal membranes and neutralizing substances in those areas and get into the circulation, then the immune system acts by a number of mechanisms to either destroy or render ineffective the offending antigen. Initially, an immune cell type called a phagocyte surrounds the infectious agent, breaks it down, and then attaches the antigenic products to its membrane. These antigens stimulate one type of T lymphocyte called a helper cell which then interacts with a several different cells that either destroy or negate the effects of the infectious agents or the cells they are infecting. Another type of lymphocyte called a B cell produces antibodies usually of the IgG class directed against the foreign antigen.

In the bone marrow, there are undifferentiated cells termed stem cells. Some of these cells get into the circulation, take on differences, and ultimately become various types of white blood cells (WBCs) or leukocytes. These differences are expressed on the surface of the WBC as identifiable leukocyte antigens, a characteristic which can be exploited to classify the cell type. This is important because the proportion of certain types of leukocytes found can be used to identify immune disease processes and responses to interventions such as exercise. For example, T cell types that help or initiate responses in other leukocytes generally have an antigen on the surface called CD4 so finding those types of cells means some sort of inflammatory process is occurring, whereas they are depressed in immunodeficiency diseases. There are other types of white blood cells as well that are largely involved in phagocytosis, regulation or repair.

Most of the diagnostic tests that evaluate an individual's immune response are designed to measure either distribution of cell types and their associated surface antigens, concentrations of substances in the bloodstream, or functional assessment of various types of leukocytes. Cell type distribution is usually determined either by taking blood from some distal or local inflammatory site and separating it into components, passing blood through a mechanized counter, or identifying characteristic antigens by their interaction with antibodies coupled to tracers that emit light. The most common soluble components related to immune response can now be quantified with commercially available immunoassays that measure the concentrations of antigens, antibodies, or immunomodulating proteins called cytokines. Typical cellular-based assays measure things like the ability of certain cell types to multiply in response to mitogenic factors, incubation of labeled tumor cells with cells that should kill them, or direct observation of phagocytes.

Levels of leukocytes circulating in the blood stream increase immediately after exercise, apparently because they are recruited from other sites; levels may spike several hours later as well. Initially, lymphocyte levels in the peripheral blood are also augmented but they become depressed within a few hours. Long term changes in white blood cell distribution have not been documented in physically active individuals. The functionality of some of these cells may be affected by exercise, however. This includes transitory suppression of natural killer cell function and changes in the ability to recruit a type of phagocytic cell called a neutrophil. Patterns of lymphocyte activation may be affected as well. The concentration of a number of cytokines is increased with exercise training. Depression of a class of antibody called IgA, which is found in the protective secretory fluids, has been observed in highly fit individuals as well. There is some suggestion that when fever accompanies illness or there is evidence of systemic involvement, exercise capacity is diminished and participation is temporarily unwise. Other evaluations have concluded that the incidence of urinary tract infections increases with high workload exercise.

Dietary supplementation with carbohydrates prior to or during exercise attenuates exhaustion and maintains sugar levels. There is some suggestion that it may also depress recruitment of white blood cells and their inflammatory factors, probably because a decline in the stress response. Certain vitamins have an antioxidant property, which means that they inhibit highly reactive destructive byproducts of oxidation. These byproducts may impair immune function in long term athletes and thus these vitamins may be useful. In the elderly population, many markers of immune function are suppressed, but it unclear whether this is due to the aging process or underlying concomitant health issues or inadequate diet. Weight loss and immune function parameters have not been adequately correlated to really assess the effects of weight reduction.

Review Video: Immune System
Visit mometrix.com/academy and enter code: 622899

HIV

Human immunodeficiency virus or HIV is typically contracted through sexual contact or intravenous drug use. Sensitive screening tests for blood donations have virtually eliminated transfusions as the source of infection. After infection, the individual presents with flu-like symptoms which resolve after a brief period. The HIV virus continues to replicate in the lymphatic system and attack helper T cells until further symptoms reemerge much later. By this time, a full-blown case of AIDS or acquired immunodeficiency syndrome has developed, generally diagnosed by depressed numbers of CD4 positive cells, recurrent infections with a variety of other microorganisms, presence of unique malignancies, and unplanned weight loss. The hallmark weight loss symptom has now preceded more toward a redistribution of weight in patients receiving these HIV drugs; fat tends to accumulate in the central region with severe wasting in their peripheral areas. Anthropometric measurements, simple timed tests to evaluate their ability to perform certain functions, neuromotor tests, viral load, CD4 levels, and targeted histories are all used for diagnosis and evaluation.

HIV is a retrovirus that contains its genetic information in RNA, thus requiring translation into DNA through an enzyme called reverse transcriptase. There are now a number of drugs used to treat HIV whose modes of action revolve around preventing HIV replication at some point, usually by inhibiting reverse transcriptase or inhibiting proteases which break down proteins. Most treatment plans call for a combination of drugs to drastically decrease the viral load. Many patients also take medications for their other opportunistic infections, drugs to arouse their desire for food, and sometimes hormones. Some may need to be fed by connection to external machinery. It is now felt that exercise programs play a vital role as well in increasing their lean muscle mass and endurance. If they have developed the fat redistribution syndrome called lipodystrophy, these programs can eliminate excess weight but may not significantly alter the pattern.

The reverse transcriptase inhibitors (RTIs) given to HIV patients are of two types, either those containing nucleosides to prevent replication or those of some other configuration. There are now plenty examples of the former nucleoside type, including zidovudine (Retrovir, also called AZT), didanosine (Videx), lamivudine (Epivir), and a combination of the latter two called Combivir. There are few nonnucleoside RTIs, including nevirapine (Viramune). The other class of HIV drug prevents protein degradation by inhibiting proteases. Examples of protease inhibitors include indinavir (Crixivan) and ritonavir (Norvir).

The emphasis during exercise testing in a patient with HIV infection is on evaluating their functional ability to perform tasks that might be incorporated into an exercise program and to address the individual's specific problems and needs. Protocols vary somewhat depending on the whether the patient is recuperating from a current bout of symptoms or is relatively stable. Anthropometric measurements are important in any category in order to determine the degree of muscle wasting in the extremities, especially the relationship between the waist and hip circumference. Usually a patient under recovery can only perform simple tests for evaluation, including typically measuring how far they can walk in 6 minutes, how fast they can get out of and back into a chair for 10 times, and simple flexibility and one repetition maximum tests. Endurance testing for a patient whose disease is currently under control can include timed abdominal crunches and the addition of less than maximal exercise. If the patient is relatively active, exercise intensity can be higher.

Use of progressive resistance training (PRT) is paramount in HIV patients because it has been found to increase the muscle mass and strength that has been lost through wasting in these individuals. A typical PRT program is designed in 3 equal segments throughout one year. Several resistance exercises directed toward different muscle groups, especially antagonistic ones and those for the lower limbs, are selected for each segment and differ somewhat by phase. One rep minimums are determined at the beginning of each phase and used to determine the submaximal workload utilized for each exercise; the most intense period is the 2 middle months of each where up to 80 percent of 1-RM might be used. The number of repetitions and sets increase during different segments. Usually the patient trains three times weekly for about ¾ of an hour except for a one-week period between phases when they do no resistance exercises but are advised to remain relatively active.

Resistance training is important to increase muscle mass for all HIV patients. Endurance training is really more important for those who have exhibited fat redistribution to the abdominal area. This is because this type of aerobic exercise has been found to decrease overall fat and possibly improve immune status. A year-long aerobic training program is very similar to PRT protocols in that it consists of three phases separated by a week of relative rest. Each month during one segment, the time spent doing aerobics on whatever machines the patient prefers is incrementally increased while the target heart rate is increased as well. Typical maximums are 25 minutes spent achieving a heart rate up to 85 percent of the reserve.

Chronic Fatigue Syndrome

Chronic fatigue syndrome (CFS) is defined as a collection of symptoms that result in protracted and incapacitating fatigue, generally for a period of at least a half year. The commencement of the symptoms can be pinpointed but the causative agent or other underlying disease cannot. The associated indicators include debilitating mental impairments to recall or focus, reduced ability to participate in daily activities, sore throat, sensitive lymphatics, various painful areas including headache, and restless sleep. Various viruses, hormonal changes, immunomodulator level changes, other diseases, and more have been investigated as causative agents but the etiology remains elusive at present. CFS is most often found in women and generally persists for about 7 years so it is very incapacitating.

Since there are no definitive causative agents for CFS, the diagnosis is really one of exclusion of other diseases. Documentation of a cluster of the types of symptoms seen in these patients is useful, but after that some sort of flow chart to eliminate the presence of other diseases is helpful. Initially, clinical evaluation including a panel of laboratory tests and neurological examinations should be done. If no other diseases are suggested, the patient is classified as having chronic fatigue syndrome if the associated symptoms are present. Usually there is further classification in terms of length and intensity of symptoms, functional ability, and concomitant illnesses. The latter are most often psychiatric in nature and small amounts of antidepressants are often prescribed. Pain relievers and various other agents are sometimes given as well. Management is directed toward alleviation of symptoms.

For the most part, studies documenting the physiological responses to exercise in patients with chronic fatigue syndrome have shown few if any abnormal reactions or inherent properties. Inherent muscle weakness has not been demonstrated in these individuals. One area of concern is the pattern of heart rate changes because (1) one study found that CFS patients had a lag in the rate of HR increase during exercise, and (2) sometimes their HR can rapidly deteriorate after exercise. Thus, they usually are attached to both heart rate and blood pressure monitors. Exercise testing should incorporate cardio and respiratory tests just to rule out those types of underlying disease. Otherwise, fairly normal testing practices can be followed.

The major goal of an exercise program for a CFS patient is at least partial restoration of the functions of daily life. Design needs to be patient-specific. Nevertheless, there are some guidelines for program design. Exercises emphasizing proper breathing techniques should be included because these patients are inclined to panic and thus breathe too rapidly. These individuals have been relatively sedentary in general so initial muscle strengthening and endurance programming should be at very low levels to avoid symptomatic bouts, and workloads should be increased at a slow pace, generally no more than once weekly. The frequency may be less than in some other programs as well. However, they should be instructed to do flexibility exercises every day. If they have a relapse, programs may need to be temporarily suspended.

Iron

In the body, iron is either stockpiled in various organs in the form of ferritin, transmitted through the circulation as transferrin, or found as an integral part of oxygenation processes in the blood or muscles. If the amount of iron taken in does not equal the amount lost through various forms of excretion or blood loss, some degree of iron deficiency results. The extreme form is iron deficiency anemia in which all types of iron are depressed, in particular the levels of iron bound to hemoglobin, the protein found in red blood cells that transports oxygen. Diets rich in iron-containing foods are important to prevent this condition, especially in women who are losing blood through menstruation. Ingestion of lean meat is the best way to add iron coupled to hemoglobin, which is the most readily utilized. Fortified cereal products and some vegetables and fruits can supply other forms of iron which are less readily absorbed.

Iron deficiency anemia presents with symptoms that are very ill-defined such as tiredness, headache, or susceptibility to infection. Thus, confirmation really needs to be done via laboratory tests to determine all bodily forms of iron such as hemoglobin concentration, levels and percentage saturation of transferrin in the serum, and ferritin concentration found in the serum. Any situation that calls for increased utilization, loss, or insufficient dietary ingestion of iron can precipitate iron loss. Of particular interest is the observation that athletes can develop anemia with excessive workloads. Any level of iron depletion might be treated by ingestion of iron pills along with vitamin C to augment its assimilation. A more controversial treatment is the inoculation of iron directly into muscles. If the individual is experiencing anemia, they should probably not exercise until more normal iron levels are present.

Sickle-Cell Anemia

Sickle-cell anemia is an inherited disease in which hemoglobin variants can result in aggregation of those molecules into a characteristic sickle shape and subsequent blockage of capillaries. The disease is most prevalent in black populations and may have originated as an adaptation to malarial infection. Sickling occurs because the amino acid changes in these variants, termed hemoglobin S, render them less able to dissolve and also less capable of oxygen saturation. Thus, these individuals have heightened difficulties in oxygen-poor environments. The condition can be exacerbated by exercise as well. If the abnormality is present on only one allele, actual presentation of this type of anemia is less likely.

Generally, if an individual possesses only one HbS allele, only laboratory tests for gene detection, ability to induce sickling, or solubility can identify the trait because these subjects rarely have symptoms. If the person is homozygous for the gene, they will usually present with symptoms of anemia, shortness of breath, an enlarged spleen, and the characteristic sickle-shaped blood cells. The latter condition may be treated with drugs that augment levels of other hemoglobin species. After exercise, their muscles may become weak and extrude important enzymes, organ failure (particularly the kidney) can occur, they often become dehydrated, and death is a real possibility if they are not closely monitored.

Education and Behavior Change

Transtheoretical Model of Change

The transtheoretical model (TTM) of behavioral change as applied to exercise centers around the idea that people need to precede through certain stages and their associated thought and action processes before they can proceed to the next stage. Thus, sedentary individuals must first weigh the advantages and disadvantages of an exercise program before they can actually begin one and the exercise professional can aid them by educating them. When they are still contemplating but appear to be more ready to begin a program, specific aspirations can be formulated based on interest. If a person is somewhat active, then laying the groundwork to step this up to optimal intensity should be begun. If they already have been optimally exercising for a short while, typically a half year or less, the next step is to ingrain the pattern into their lifestyle. Finally, ways to ensure long-term adherence to the program should be instituted by finding ways to keep it interesting and social and to prevent relapses, or returns to prior less active patterns.

Social Cognitive Theory

Social cognitive theory (SCT) is based on the concept that behavioral modifications occur because of the right combination the type of activity, the individual's unique current and previous history, and the milieu surrounding the activity. According to SCT, in order to accomplish change such as beginning or intensifying an exercise program, the individual must feel that they are capable of accomplishing the goals that are set forth. Thus, new challenging goals are important but should be incorporated incrementally. When the person perceives that they are mastering one step or if they are shown that others can perform the task, they are given impetus to proceed further. Social cognitive theory also emphasizes the promising results of participation in the activity, including not only the health benefits but also the communal and self-worth aspects. The latter appears to play an important role because it has been found that feelings of self-worth and mastery influence the choice of activities and adherence to programs.

Anxiety Disorders

There are several different types of anxiety disorders, all more prevalent in women, which tend to be unremitting instead of acute responses. They all basically involve exaggerated fears and anxieties. Involuntary stress reactions such as sweating and shaking are activated. If the trigger and duration is rapid, the disorder is usually a panic attack. If the individual worries incessantly and somewhat needlessly, they are said to have a generalized anxiety disorder. Other variations involve the fanatical performance of certain activities, mental replaying of a traumatic event, or unusual levels of reticence in social circumstances. In addition to antidepressive medications, drugs called benzodiazepines are often given to suppress symptoms and a number of psychological techniques are used. Exercise programs should not have any adverse effects on these patients.

Eating Disorders

There are primarily three different types of eating disorders. Two of them are derived from unhappiness with body weight (usually unrealistic) and desire for weight loss. In anorexia nervosa, the individual refuses to consume enough calories to maintain a suitable body weight, thus becoming very thin and exposing themselves to a variety of abnormalities including bone loss and heart problems that can result in mortality. In another variant, bulimia nervosa, the person eats often ravenously but then uses extraordinary methods to flush out the consumed food, thus resulting in susceptibility to severe gastrointestinal problems in particular. There are also people who have periods where they eat quickly and obsessively without considering need; in other words, they binge eat. Treatment for each disorder involves nutritional counseling and targeted exercise programs as well as some sort of psychological intervention.

Substance Abuse and Dependence

When an individual abuses a substance such as alcohol or certain drugs, they become unable to shoulder their responsibilities of daily life such as work or social obligations. If this use proceeds to dependence, the typical presentation also includes the necessity for increased amounts of the substance to satisfy their cravings, measurable adverse signs if the material is unavailable, and evidence of mental incapacity or actual loss of consciousness. In addition to individualized rehabilitation programs, there are a number of substance abuse groups that these individuals can join.

Health Belief Model and Social Ecology Theory

In the health belief model, it is postulated that people institute health-related changes because they want to prevent disease. They do not tend to alter their lifestyle unless they feel they are at risk for the ailment, that the disease is justifiably serious, that proposed activities will help them, and there are no significant obstacles to participation. The social ecology theory has a different emphasis, mainly which the entire atmosphere under which the change occurs influences the probability of success. In other words, the physical surroundings where the individual will perform the activity or exercise are important, but so are self-perceived barriers to or benefits of participation as well as outside interactions with other people or bureaucracy.

Reasoned Action and Planned Behavior

The theory of reasoned action has not been well-studied but it is based on the premise that all actions are preceded by purposeful intent. The theory of planned behavior (TPB) is an extrapolation of this model. Here the belief is that an individual will change their behavior if they first formulate the plan to do so because they are somehow motivated, they perceive the activity positively, and they feel that they are capable of controlling the action themselves. The utility of these theories has not unequivocally proven but components of them may provide impetus for certain individuals.

Exercise Participation

Exercise participation rates depend to a large extent on the attitudes of the individual, but there are some generalizations. Men tend to engage in more intense activities than women, who tend to prefer more restrained things like fast walking. As people age, they tend to engage in less stressful physical pursuits. Positive associations between number of years of school completed as well as income level and the level of activity have been demonstrated as well. Health club membership, for example, is skewed toward highly educated, high wage earners. Extremely overweight individuals have low participation rates, which creates a cyclical problem of reinforcement of the weight issue. In addition, the presence of disease is associated with sedentary lifestyle and rate of relapse in established exercise programs.

Physical activities or exercises must be available in opportune locations, at suitable times, and in readily available and enjoyable modes to increase adherence to a program. Adherence is basically the percentage of recommended movement that is actually performed. At the beginning, this could just mean making simple lifestyle adjustments, and after that small stepwise changes are most effective. If for example, the individual is participating in a group class, various ways to perform an exercise can be demonstrated to account for inter-individual variability. Reasonable objectives should be established. In addition, incentives and encouragement have been found to be great motivators for exercise participation, especially during the early phases of a program. Sometimes it is even helpful to sign informal agreements where the individual pledges to particular goals with rewards when these are achieved. The exercise professional should not only provide encouragement and positive feedback, but they should also be role models and perform some of the activities along with their subject.

One way to enhance maintenance of an exercise program after supervision is terminated is for the exercise professional to connect the activity performed to something similar that the individual can do on their own. In other words, the person must already be incorporating other activities outside the supervised environment that mimic the program and can be self-performed at home or elsewhere. All the other aspects such as setting goals need to be constantly reassessed. There is also an interviewing technique that the health professional can utilize whereby they stress free will coupled with the benefits of maintenance to motivate the individual; this practice has been found to be particularly useful for people with substance abuse problems.

Working with Individual Patients

The exercise professional needs to take an individualized approach to each patient and find ways to create a positive relationship with them. They need to initially sit down with the client and have them talk about their issues in a manner that indicates a personal interest and understanding of their problems. This involves responding to them in a way that they know you have been listening well enough to understand the subliminal intent of their conversation. When developing an exercise program for clients, the professional should never give advice; instead they need to provide constructive information for decision making, and strategies for overcoming any barriers. A problem can only be solved if it is recognized and various solutions are outlined and weighed before they are implemented. Every effort to increase their confidence level, called self-efficacy, quantify aspirations, and remove barriers to later non-compliance should be made.

LIFESTYLE MANAGEMENT

Different choices that individuals make have a significant impact on their overall state of health. By offering lifestyle management services, the exercise physiologist may help the patient to improve his overall health. Ideally such improvements may reduce the need for intrusive measures like drugs or surgery. Lifestyle management services may also reduce the risk of sudden death. Lifestyle management services include assistance and counseling with smoking cessation, improvement of dietary decisions, and improvements in physical fitness. This list does not exhaust the possibilities. Lifestyle management services are an integral part of the exercise physiologist's services. Below are three main lifestyle choices:

- Fitness—Staying physically fit helps the entire body to work better. Blood flows better, the heart is more efficient, muscles and bones are stronger, and organs function better. Physical fitness also helps people to maintain a healthy body weight, and good weight management is key to good health. Physical fitness does not necessarily come from exercise alone—it also comes from participating in recreational activities and making choices that result in physical activity.
- Nutrition—Eating habits are key to a healthy lifestyle. Someone who overeats and who eats primarily processed food does not give his body the nutrients it needs for optimal health. Portion control and eating fresh or minimally processed foods are important lifestyle choices.
- Habits—Habits like smoking or excessive drinking can quickly derail a person's health. Positive habits can enhance a person's health.

HEART RATE VARIABILITY

Research shows that heart rate variability (the difference between heart rate during inhalation and exhalation) is different depending on certain lifestyle choices. The heart rate variability is important because a greater variability indicates greater vagal tone. Research has found that people who are physically fit have higher variability between inhalations and exhalations than do those who smoke or have a sedentary lifestyle. This indicates that moving from a sedentary lifestyle to a more active lifestyle or discontinuing smoking can help improve vagal tone. Reduced vagal tone is associated with higher risks of mortality due to cardiovascular causes. These lifestyle changes can help to improve heart health by improving vagal tone.

LONG-TERM COMMITMENT

One of the hardest parts of creating an exercise program for a patient is developing one to which the patient can commit over the long term. There are strategies you can impart to your patients that will help increase their chances of success. First, discuss the many different possible ways she can become more physically active. Helping your patient to find activities she enjoys and helping her recognize that there are a variety of things she can do will help take the perceived boredom out of exercise. Also, discuss footwear and clothing choices with your patients—comfort is an important part of an exercise program. Shoes are especially important. Help your patient to create a schedule in order to be sure that she makes time to be physically active most days of the week.

In addition to variety and fun, comfortable clothing and shoes, and making exercise a priority, you can also help your patient by encouraging her to use music in her exercise routines. Music can make exercise more enjoyable, and it can also help the patient keep track of how long she has been working out. Encourage your patient to discuss her fitness goals with supportive friends and family. People that will encourage her and hold her accountable in a positive way will add to her motivation to continue with her program. Help your patient to set realistic and healthy goals. Overdoing it can cause discomfort or even injury—a sure way to derail your patient's goals. Remind your patient to reward herself along the way. Small rewards as she achieves significant steps toward her goal can help her stay enthusiastic about what she is doing.

Attitude

The way that a patient looks at lifestyle changes such as becoming more physically active can make a big difference in his level of success. The first step toward helping your patient achieve his goals is to help him get into the right mindset. First, encourage your patient to spend time visualizing what he wants to achieve. Suggest to your patient that he think about the ultimate benefits of lifestyle changes. Next, help your patient to recognize self-criticism and self-destructive thoughts. We all make excuses not to do the things that are good for us. Teach your patients to answer back to those criticisms and excuses with positive statements and solutions. Help your patient to set achievable goals. Setting unrealistic goals can leave your patient feeling overwhelmed. By setting realistic goals, success becomes possible. Suggest to your patient that he write his goals down. Finally, whenever working towards goals, it is important to be prepared for setbacks. Remind patients to commit to being persistent.

Stress

The human body reacts to stress typically by releasing the hormones adrenaline and cortisol into the system. These hormones give the body extra strength, endurance, and focus for dealing with emergencies. However, the usual sources of stress in today's society do not often require this kind of fight-or-flight reaction. Many of the sources of stress are ongoing and therefore cause cortisol levels to become chronically elevated. This can lead to higher blood pressure, higher fasting glucose levels, and a poorly functioning immune system. Thus, stress management is an important part of lifestyle management services. The exercise physiologist can help the patient develop healthy coping strategies for countering the negative effects of stress—deep breathing, meditation, massage, counseling, stretching, hobbies, and exercise are all effective means to reduce stress.

Emotional Stress and Chronic Diseases

Stress, depression, and anxiety can all be linked to heart disease and other chronic diseases. Ongoing stress triggers the production of cortisol in the body, which can contribute to weight gain and other problems. Acute moments of stress can trigger cardiac events. Depression and anxiety are common reactions to chronic disease. Heart disease patients are three times as likely as the general population to struggle with depression. Severe anxiety and hostility have been linked to a higher risk of heart disease.

Emotional/mental conditions can contribute to disease, and disease can trigger the development of these conditions. It is important to recognize the signs of depression, anxiety, and stress. These things can derail an exercise program if left unaddressed. At the same time, exercise is one of the best ways to treat these conditions.

Social support: Support from other people plays a large role in the health and well-being of people with heart disease or other diseases. Those who have robust social support tend to fare better when facing a disease. Studies have found that people without a good social network are more likely to die after a cardiac event. They also don't respond as well to treatment regimens. For the purpose of discussion, social support can be divided into two categories: structural support and functional support. Structural support refers to the patient's social life—whether or not they are married, whether they have close friends and family, and whether they are involved in any structured organizations. Functional support refers to how supported the person feels. A patient who has someone to help with daily activities and who has someone to talk to about what she is going through has good functional support.

Nutrition

Ten nutritional tips that will promote better health are as follows:

- Eat breakfast. Eating breakfast first thing in the morning helps to give the metabolism a boost. It also promotes insulin sensitivity and can help to lower blood pressure.
- Choose healthy snacks. Snacking on a piece of fruit or some vegetables like carrots, celery, or cucumbers is a great start. If you mix the produce with a snack that contains fat and/or protein it will fill you up better. Try an apple and cheese or celery sticks and peanut butter.
- Chew your food thoroughly. Chewing is the first step to good digestion. Take the time to really chew and enjoy your food.
- Up your fiber intake. Getting enough fiber is associated with good digestion. When digestion works well your body gets more nutrients from your food and you feel better. Good fiber intake also helps to lower the risk of heart disease.

- Mind your portions. For each meal, your protein portion should be about the size of a deck of cards. Your vegetable and/or grain portions should be about the size of your fist.
- Eat more fish. The omega three fatty acids in cold-water fish are associated with a lower risk of heart disease, fewer joint problems, and a better sense of well being.
- Eat more than five servings of fruits and vegetables each day. Five is the bare minimum—aim to eat more produce.
- Embrace balance. You can still enjoy a sweet, salty, or even a deep-fried snack now and again. Just don't overdo.
- Use good fats. Fat sources like olive oil have a good balance of polyunsaturated and monounsaturated fat. They promote good heart health.
- Choose fresh foods. One of the best ways to improve eating habits is to eat at home more and to avoid prepackaged, processed foods. Fresh meats, dairy, fruits, vegetables, and breads are the best choices for good health.

Water Intake

The human body needs regular water intake in order to function at its best. If the body becomes mildly dehydrated, the individual is likely to experience sluggishness or headaches. Moderate to severe dehydration is uncommon but can result in serious health issues.

When an individual begins an exercise program, his body needs more water because it uses more water. It is important that an exercise physiologist help his patients to recognize the importance of water intake, as well as the signs of dehydration.

The commonly recommended amount of water intake is eight 8oz glasses each day, but individual needs do vary. A better guide may be one half ounce of water per pound of body weight per day. Thirst, dry mouth, dark colored urine, and lightheadedness are all signs of early dehydration.

Diet and Exercise

Modifications in the diet are an effective way to lose weight. By eating more nutritious foods and restricting calorie intake, a person can lose weight at a safe pace. Weight loss through diet alone does not necessarily address body composition beyond eliminating pounds.

Exercise is another safe way to create a calorie deficit, which can lead to weight loss. Exercise can also help to modify body composition. Resistance training helps to build muscle and cardiorespiratory training helps the body to burn fat.

Together, exercise and diet make the most sense when a person wishes to modify her body composition. First, a healthy diet will support any exercise efforts. It can also promote weight loss if calorie intake is appropriate. Exercise helps modify the body's lean mass and fat percentage to a healthier composition.

Government Recommended Food Pyramid

Recently, the United States government updated the food pyramid to include the new understanding of the role that fat and protein play in a healthy diet.

The new food pyramid is actually tailored to a person's age, sex, body mass index, and activity level. It recommends that each person get a variety of foods each day from grains, vegetables, fruits, healthy fats like olive oil, dairy products, and meats and beans.

A general range is six to eight servings of grains each day with half being from whole grain sources; three cups of vegetables each day; two to three cups of fruit each day; three servings of dairy each day; and around six ounces of protein from meats and beans. The food pyramid also emphasizes the need for physical activity—30 to 90 minutes a day depending on the individual's health needs.

Nutritional Therapies

Obese: For someone who has metabolic syndrome or who is obese, one therapeutic goal is to lose weight at a safe and reasonable rate. Generally, this is considered to be 1 to 2 pounds per week. Other goals include lowering risk factors for heart disease and achieving a healthy BMI. Nutritional recommendations include reducing calorie intake by up to 1000 calories a day, eating less than 30 percent of daily calories from fat, and eating less than 300 mg of cholesterol a day. Also, the patient should aim for 2400 mg of sodium, between 1000 and 1500 mg of calcium, and at least 25 grams of fiber.

Higher risk individuals should pay more attention to the kinds of fat they consume, limiting saturated fat to less than 7% of intake, and getting up to 10% of calories from polyunsaturated fats and up to 20% of calories from monounsaturated fats.

A dietitian can help both groups of patients achieve healthy results.

Hypertensive: For the hypertensive patient, therapeutic goals include maintaining or improving blood pressure levels and reducing other cardiovascular risk factors. Ideally, the hypertensive patient will reach a blood pressure at or below 140/90 mm Hg. Specific dietary changes can help to achieve these goals. Patients at a normal weight should aim to consume an appropriate number of calories each day, which is dependent on levels of activity. Men should limit alcoholic drinks to two per day or less; women should limit alcoholic drinks to one or fewer each day. Reducing sodium intake and eating less red meat can also help to reduce high blood pressure. The patient should also be advised to get adequate amounts of calcium, magnesium, potassium, and fiber.

Cardiovascular Disease: The therapeutic goals for a patient with heart disease include lowering heart disease risk factors and lowering weight. Ideally, the patient with heart disease or at high risk for the condition will lower his total cholesterol to 160 mg/dL or less. LDL cholesterol levels should be 100 mg/dL for high-risk patients, and HDL cholesterol should be at least 40 mg/dL for men and 50 mg/dL for women. Good dietary habits can help to reduce the risk of heart disease. The patient with heart disease should limit sodium intake to 2400 mg or less per day. Fat calories should make up 30% or less of the total daily calories. Saturated fats should be kept at 10 percent or less of total daily calories. The patient should also consume foods rich in fiber and antioxidants.

DIABETES: The therapeutic goals for a patient with diabetes include achieving and maintaining a healthy weight and controlling blood sugar levels. Good dietary choices can help to achieve these goals. Carbohydrates and monounsaturated fatty acids should make up 60-70% of the daily caloric intake for a diabetic patient. Protein should make up 15-20%, and total fat should be less than 30%. Saturated fat intake should be limited to 10% of daily calories or less. The diabetic patient should also limit alcohol intake to two drinks or less per day for men, and one drink or less per day for women. Blood glucose levels should be closely monitored throughout the day.

Saturated and Unsaturated Fats

There are many types of dietary fats. They include cholesterol, saturated fat, polyunsaturated fat, and monounsaturated fat. Dietary cholesterol does contribute to increases in total cholesterol for some people. Saturated fats are fat molecules that are bonded with all the hydrogen molecules possible. High saturated fat intake can increase both LDL and HDL cholesterol levels. Polyunsaturated fat has multiple "open" bonds where a hydrogen molecule could be, but isn't. Many plant oils like sunflower oil and soybean oil are high in polyunsaturated fat. Monounsaturated fat has one "open" bond. It is also known to have a protective effect on the heart. Dietary sources include olive oil and canola oil.

Omega-3 Fatty Acids and Omega-6 Fatty Acids

Essential fatty acids are fatty acids that are necessary to good health but that the human body cannot manufacture on its own. People therefore need to get them from foods. There are two primary essential fatty acids that people need to eat. The first is omega-3 fatty acid, found in flaxseed, nuts, and coldwater, oily fish. The second is omega-6 fatty acid, found in plant-based oil like corn oil and soybean oil. Ideally, people should get somewhere between a one-to-one and a two-to-one ratio of omega-6 and omega-3 fatty acids. Omega-3 fatty acid intake is associated with a lower risk of heart disease.

Trans Fats

Trans fats are polyunsaturated fats that have been chemically processed to hold more hydrogen than they would in their natural state. These fats increase heart disease risk by raising LDL cholesterol while lowering HDL cholesterol. Studies have shown that as little as one gram of trans fat a day can significantly boost the risk of heart disease. These altered fats are found in processed foods—they help to prolong shelf life. When reading labels, check for partially or fully hydrogenated oils. These contain trans fats. Labeling requirements now force manufacturers to list trans fat content. However, foods that contain half a gram of trans fat or less per serving can claim to be free of trans fats.

Phytochemicals

Phytochemicals are the micronutrients found in fruits and vegetables that can help to prevent cancer. Different phytochemicals lower the risks of different kinds of cancers. Some examples of phytochemicals are ascorbic acid, beta-carotene, coumarin, ellagic acid, indole-3-carbinol, lutein, lycopene, organosulfur compounds, and quercetin. Leafy, green vegetables and citrus fruits are a good source of ascorbic acid. Cruciferous vegetables like broccoli and cauliflower provide indole-3-carbinole. Tomatoes are an excellent source of lycopene. And organosulfur compounds are found in onions and garlic. To get a broad range of phytochemicals, eat a wide variety of colorful fruits and vegetables.

Grains

Many people eat more calories from grains than they need to. It is easy to misjudge serving sizes when it comes to grains. For example, a full-sized bagel contains two or three servings of grain, but many people think of it as a single serving. Remind patients to read labels and check the serving size. When it comes to grains, whole grains are best. They are higher in fiber and nutrients than the refined grains found in many baked goods. To increase whole grain servings, recommend that your patients switch from wheat or white bread to 100 percent whole wheat bread. Also recommend whole grain cereals. Oatmeal is a good source of whole grain, too.

Fruits and Vegetables

Fruits and vegetables are excellent sources of carbohydrates, vitamins, phytochemicals, and fiber. Many people do not eat enough fruits and vegetables during the day. Also, most people don't eat a wide variety, instead sticking to a few favorites. To improve nutrition, recommend that patients eat at least five servings of fruits and vegetables a day and remind them to seek out a wide variety. Fruits and vegetables make excellent snacks, which is one good way to increase intake. Also encourage patients to double up on vegetables at dinner and to choose fruit as a dessert.

Protein

Protein is available from a wide variety of sources. Meat, eggs, and dairy all provide complete sources of protein. Beans, nuts, grains, and soy products also contain protein, although they do not provide a complete source of protein on their own. Suggest that your patients choose lean cuts of meat and trim the fat before cooking. Recommend that your patients remove the skin from poultry. Also, fish is an important source of many nutrients and an excellent source of protein. Encourage patients to eat fish at least once a week. Also, encourage your patients to eat one or two meatless meals a week, if not more. Beans or legumes can make a good substitute. Dairy products are another good source of protein and nutrients. Encourage patients to eat three servings of low-fat dairy per day.

Adequate Energy Intake

A program that maintains weight will balance the amount of calories consumed during a day with the amount of calories burned by natural metabolism and physical activity. To lose weight an individual must burn more calories during the day than he consumes. This is referred to as a calorie deficit. While losing weight, it is reasonable for an individual to restrict the calories consumed, but care must be used so that adequate energy is still available for the body to perform its regular functions. The body needs micronutrients in order to be at its best, and the individual runs the risk of micronutrient deficiencies during calorie restriction. There are several ways to determine the body's energy needs. One simple method multiplies the individual's body weight by ten to approximate the resting metabolic rate. Other more complex methods measure the actual calorie intake and use of the body during the day.

Program Administration

Obtaining Informed Consent

Informed consent is the practice of conveying to the participant the details of a procedure and its risks. It is actually a type of contract or agreement between the client and healthcare provider. The contract can be either written or in some cases verbal. Rules vary slightly by state. However, to give consent the individual must be of sound mind including ability to understand what they are being told. They either need to be of legal age or else a guardian of appropriate age needs to give consent. There are some instances where this consent must be in written form. These center on the disclosure of patient information to other healthcare professionals and are covered primarily by the Health Information Portability and Accountability Act. Because exercise professionals interact with other medical professionals, in general written informed consent is best.

Negligence and Malpractice

Negligence is a legal term for the failure to provide the proper and reasonable level of care according to some standard of practice. Malpractice is an extension of this concept in which the standard has been well-established for a distinct group of professionals. Both of these terms fall into the broader category of tort law governs civil damages. In the healthcare setting, the number of liable professional groups has been expanding beyond the traditional doctor or dentist because of the increasing use of certification procedures and establishment of standards and guidelines for practice. Thus, an exercise physiologist could be accused of negligence or malpractice. Ways to avoid culpability include inclusion of language on release forms that absolve the healthcare provider of responsibility, and this type of wording is now often included in exercise settings. Insurance is now available for exercise physiologists.

Communication with Clients

There are various ways of communicating information with a client, and the exercise physiologist must find out which types of communication will be most beneficial for the client. Talking with the client over the phone is most beneficial if the client can be reached easily via telephone, although the exercise physiologist needs to understand the protocol of the fitness center for making such calls from her personal number. Depending on the fitness facility, email and text reminders for appointments can be appropriate if done through a business email or contact number. The exercise physiologist needs to be careful about sending personal information regarding the client through these avenues. Additionally, keeping an updated newsletter or website can be a means of communicating mass information to several clients; however, some clients may not use these sources as a general rule.

Verbal and Nonverbal Communication

Communication throughout the exercise session is both verbal and nonverbal. The exercise physiologist should give verbal instructions and encouragement to the client while also realizing that her body language will impact the client as well. It is important to make eye contact with the client and speak kindly and confidently to him so he understands that his exercise physiologist views his time and effort as important. The exercise physiologist should maintain a professional appearance at all times, maintaining a pleasant facial expression and keeping her attention focused on the client throughout the session.

Active Listening

Active listening means that the exercise physiologist is listening to what the client has to say, looking at the client while she speaks, and asking questions at appropriate times to be sure of what the client means. Examples of active listening would be making eye contact with the client, jotting down notes regarding what the client is saying, ensuring he understands the client's request ("So what I understand you to mean is..."), and making any necessary changes to the workout routine based on the client's feedback.

Auditory, Visual, and Kinesthetic Learning Styles

An auditory learner can learn best through hearing something taught verbally; a visual learner needs to see something modeled for him; a kinesthetic learner needs to try something to understand it better. Typically, clients will have more than one learning style, and the style may vary between the different types of resistance training and cardiovascular training. One way to ensure the client has the best chance of understanding what is needed for a movement pattern is to describe the movement, model the movement for the client, then have the client complete a practice movement without any weight, or through a partial range of motion if the movement requires body weight as resistance.

Feedback

Feedback can be given to a client in a variety of ways. Evaluative feedback helps the client know what she is doing correctly and incorrectly in the movement pattern ("You are doing a great job of not allowing your knees to go past your toes, but make sure your toes are pointed forward."). Supportive feedback is a means of encouraging the client, perhaps through a difficult part of the workout ("I know it's tough, but we're almost through. Do you think you can finish 2 more laps?"). Descriptive feedback is clear and concise feedback that provides correction at the end of a movement pattern or session ("In future squat-type exercises, I want you to focus on squeezing the muscles of your gluteus to decrease pressure on your knees."). Feedback should be given to the client verbally at regular intervals, but also in written form when she is regularly evaluated for goal assessment.

Emergency Medical Plans

Any physical fitness facility must have developed an emergency care plan to deal with serious unplanned events or health changes indicating injury or illness. Any employee who performs or supervises exercise testing or programs needs to be qualified to administer basic cardiopulmonary resuscitation (CPR) and if possible, they should be further trained in advanced cardiac life support (ACLS) techniques. A minimum of one individual trained in the latter procedures as well as a doctor should be reachable during maximum testing protocols. There should be clearly defined and visible emergency procedures and phone numbers. Emergency equipment should be tested and maintained regularly and procedures for doing so should be reviewed by all employees at least 4 times a year. Support teams should be in intimate contact with the group and immediately called in emergencies. In addition, there are a number of pieces of equipment and pharmacologic agents that should be kept in the facility.

CPR and ACLS

Unless the exercise professional is additionally licensed to perform CPR or ACLS techniques, they really do not have legal authority to perform them and should defer to those individuals who do. CPR or cardiopulmonary resuscitation involves clearing the patient's airways to listen for breathing and then alternating series of compressions with mouth-to-mouth resuscitation. If this does not work, defibrillation should be attempted, which shocks the heart. If no signs of circulation are present after three shocks, the two techniques can be alternated. The emergency medical system should always be activated for this presentation as well as many other cardiac, pulmonary and diabetic symptoms.

Emergency Equipment and Drugs

An emergency plan and some equipment are both necessary in any facility outside the home that provides fitness equipment for patron or patient use. One of the most important pieces of emergency equipment that must be available at a fitness facility is an automated external defibrillator or manual version that delivers an electric shock to the heart to control a fluttering heartbeat. Posted instructions regarding access to defibrillation equipment are either suggested or required as the environment shifts toward a supervised clinical exercise program. A blood pressure cuff and stethoscope is essential. Oxygen and ways to administer it if needed should be readily available. Intravenous fluids and associated equipment, suctioning gear, and other first aid supplies should be in stock. A phone line is always required. A plan to call the EMS (emergency medical services) at 911 or elsewhere should be in place. There are several different types of drugs that need to be available. The majority of these are related to the restoration of normal cardiac responses, including agents to treat rapid or slow heart beats, restore proper rhythm, reestablish a pulse, and treat episodes of acute chest pain to prevent a heart attack. The list is quite long in each category but some essential drugs include aspirin and nitroglycerin to prevent heart attacks, epinephrine or atropine to restore and regulate the pulse, and agents like lidocaine to reestablish proper rhythm patterns.

Cardiovascular life support drugs are numerous and many should be available in any exercise facility or clinical environment. One type of drug inhibits the angiotensin-converting enzyme (ACE inhibitors) such as enalapril (Vasotec) and many of these are given in combination with diuretics like hydrochlorothiazide. Drugs that suppress the beta receptors in the heart are common like propranolol (Inderal) but again are often combined with diuretics. There are a number of agents that restrict calcium movement in heart and arterial muscle and widen the arteries; these are called calcium channel blockers with one of the most common being some version of verapamil (Calan). Drugs that break down fibrin such as streptokinase should be available, as should vasodilators like nitroglycerin. The list is too extensive to quote in its entirety.

Legal and Professional Considerations

Stratifying Client Risk and Obtaining Medical Clearance to Minimize Negligence

Negligence is defined as the breach of the duty of care between a professional and a client. If an exercise physiologist doesn't take time to stratify client risk and obtain medical clearance if indicated, she will be seen as negligent should anything happen to the client during the course of exercise programming. The exercise physiologist is obligated to do everything in her power to ensure the client is exercising in a safe environment with minimal risk to health and well-being; stratifying client risk and obtaining medical clearance meets this professional requirement.

Levels of Risk Stratification

The Health History Questionnaire enables clients to see specifically which risk factors affect them. For instance, the following risk factors could indicate coronary artery disease: hypertension, family history, high cholesterol, cigarette smoking, impaired fasting glucose, obesity, sedentary lifestyle. Additionally, risk factors can also be assessed during the exercise session. The following risk factors could indicate pulmonary, metabolic, or cardiovascular disease: pain or tension in chest, neck, jaws, arms, or other areas; dizziness; shortness of breath; orthopnea or nightly dyspnea; palpitations; ankle edema; known heart murmur; intermittent claudication; unusual fatigue or shortness of breath during normal activities. Clients can be stratified as low, moderate, or high risk based upon the aforementioned symptoms.

Medical Clearance Requirements

If a client answers yes to one or more questions indicating cardiovascular or metabolic or pulmonary disease and has a history of chronic disease, medical clearance is necessary to begin treatment through exercise. If a client answers yes to one or more of these questions, the exercise physiologist should take into account the health history as it is described by the client and should use his best judgment in recommending medical clearance or not. Generally, if the client was just barely placed in the moderate-risk category, but could be in the high-risk category very soon, medical clearance might be a good idea. Additionally, if the client responds poorly in the exercise testing, especially if she is unable to catch her breath or experiences heart palpitations, medical clearance is necessary.

Supervision for Individuals Who Received Medical Clearance

Clients who have received medical clearance for exercise should be monitored continually during the exercise session. Additionally, they need to indicate how hard they feel they are working according to the RPE scale. These clients should never be left alone to exercise until they have come to a point where their risk factors are decreasing or it is deemed that they can exercise safely by themselves.

Continuing Education

An exercise physiologist should keep abreast of changes and modifications within the field by attending regular continuing education. This can be done through taking classes that help to maintain certification or by receiving a degree in higher education. Training can be hands on, online, or in a classroom setting. The important thing is for the physiologist to consider how this education will benefit her knowledge so that clients can ultimately benefit from it. The physiologist should take classes that directly relate to the populations that she trains.

Effective Communication with Allied Professionals

If a client requires medical clearance to participate in a workout program, or has been referred to an exercise physiologist by a medical professional, it is appropriate to regularly communicate about the client's progress. The ideal ways for this to happen are through phone calls or postal service. Sensitive information should never be given through email or left on an answering machine, in order to protect patient privacy. The client also needs to be fully aware that information is being shared, and in the appropriate instances, sign a release of information.

Effective Relationships with Individuals in the Greater Health Community

The exercise physiologist should always be aware that there are many different people invested in seeing a community grow in health and wellness. It would be to the exercise physiologist's benefit to network with like-minded medical and allied health professionals in the community by attending professional events and creating a strong referral system for clients to seek additional help that is outside the exercise physiologist's scope of practice. The physiologist can partner with other professionals to provide special package pricing combined with other professional services. Being active in the community and attending community health events is the best way for exercise physiologists to network with other health practitioners to reach a common goal.

Recommending Other Health Services

When an exercise physiologist realizes that a client needs help in areas outside the physiologist's scope of practice, the client needs to be referred. For instance, if a client needs more detailed information to help him nutritionally than is provided by the general guidelines found on www.myplate.gov, the client should be referred to a dietitian. If a client struggles excessively with finding solutions to stress management, and general guidelines for relaxation do not seem to suffice, the client should be referred to a life coach for further guidance.

CPR and AED

An exercise physiologist should maintain a current CPR/AED certification at all times. If a client becomes unconscious or stops breathing at any time, CPR protocol should be initiated. AED protocol should be initiated as necessary if there is more than one person at hand in a situation where a client collapses. If an exercise physiologist does not maintain a current CPR/AED certification, she could be held liable for practicing without a license.

Emergency Procedures Clearly Delineated for the Client

The exercise physiologist should make clear to the client proper procedure in case of emergencies. For instance, in case of a fire or inclement weather, the client should know where the exits are or where to seek adequate shelter. Whenever the fitness facility updates its procedures, it is the exercise physiologist's responsibility to ensure the client knows what to do. Additionally, the exercise physiologist should have on file permission from the client to call emergency services or a medical practitioner if appropriate.

Basic First-Aid Procedures

Exercise Intolerance

If a client is experiencing exercise intolerance, a cooldown should be initiated immediately to bring the client's heart rate back down to resting levels. The client needs to drink adequate amounts of water to maintain hydration. The client should continue moving as necessary until heart rate returns to normal. If the client feels dizzy or overheated, he can sit down, but lying down is contraindicated. The client should be given some cool water, and a cold towel or compress should be applied to his neck to reduce body temperature. If the client is having trouble breathing due to chest pains, medical personnel should be contacted as it may be exercise-induced angina.

Exercise-Related Injury

If the client has an exercise-related injury, the client should be put in a sitting position and RICE (rest, ice, compression, elevation) should be followed for the injured area as needed. A medical practitioner should be immediately called. This information should be kept on file prior to any exercise sessions taking place so it can be accessed in the event of an emergency. The exercise physiologist should also have on file a client's permission to call emergency services in the event of an emergency if it's deemed necessary.

Client Safety in the Fitness Facility

Client safety can be ensured by having them engage in exercises that correspond to their current fitness level. Clients should also be taught how to correctly handle resistance machines and free weights to avoid personal injury. They should also be made aware of facility rules regarding flow of traffic inside the facility, appropriate cardiovascular machine usage, and age requirements for using equipment. Clients should never use a machine they do not know how to use; this can be remedied by the exercise physiologist giving a comprehensive education on machine usage.

Injuries

There are several injuries that can be common complaints of clients, and it is beneficial for exercise physiologists to know how to work around them during an exercise session. Shin splints are characterized by pain along the outside of the leg starting right below the knee. A sprain is pain in the joint where a ligament has been overstretched. A strain is characterized by muscle fibers tearing because of being overstretched. Bursitis is inflammation of the bursa sacs. Tendonitis is inflammation or irritation of a tendon. A fracture is a break in a bone. Patello-femoral pain syndrome is localized pain in front of the knee. Low back pain is localized pain across the lower back in the lumbar spine and pelvis. Plantar fasciitis is inflammation of the fascia on the bottom of the foot and often results in heel pain and tenderness.

If shin splints, sprain, or strain occur during the course of exercise, ice should be applied immediately and the ankle or other joint elevated. The client should be encouraged to wrap the area in a compression sleeve and visit a medical professional. If a fracture occurs, medical help should be sought immediately. A client with bursitis and tendonitis should engage in non–weight-bearing cardiovascular activities, and resistance activities should utilize resistance bands. If a client has patello-femoral pain syndrome, medical clearance should be given prior to exercise, and non–weight-bearing cardiovascular activity should be the focus. Resistance activities should be focused around machine weights. For low back pain and plantar fasciitis, the warm-up and stretch segments should be extended, and myofascial release techniques should be utilized.

Contraindications to Exercises of the Major Muscle Groups

Even though some resistance exercises may be beneficial for many of the healthy population, they may be contraindicated in certain populations. For example, straight leg sit-ups and standing bent-over toe touches lose their exercise value for some people with neck and back issues because it places high compressional forces on the spinal column. Double leg raises can cause hyperextension of the lower back and place unnecessary stress on it, which is especially unneeded for clients who already have low back problems. Clients who are obese or have knee issues can cause undue stress by performing full squats. Overall, the exercise physiologist needs to assess potential exercise risk against reward when choosing exercises for the client.

Liability During Emergency Procedures

When an emergency situation happens and the client is directly under the exercise physiologist's supervision, the exercise physiologist is held liable for what happens to the client. The exercise physiologist is responsible for the client's safety while performing exercise, and if an emergency occurs within the fitness facility, the physiologist must do her best to ensure the client's safety. The physiologist must be up-to-date on fitness emergency procedures.

Common Musculoskeletal Injuries

When a client is not fit, there are some common musculoskeletal injuries that might take place. Although a physiologist may do his best to monitor the client, there may be pre-existing weakness that predisposes the client to injury. Some common injuries are as follows: contusion (bruising) of the muscle, sprain or strain of the muscle, fracture (including stress fractures with overuse or poor footwear) of the bones. The client must also be aware of any predispositions to injury and know what to do about an acute injury if she is exercising on her own.

Management and First-Aid During Exercise

Common Cardiovascular Complications

If a cardiovascular event happens during an exercise session, the exercise physiologist needs to be aware of signs and symptoms that indicate it. The signs and symptoms are as follows: chest pain (or in head, neck, jaw, or arms), heart palpitations, hyperventilation, syncope, dyspnea, unusual shortness of breath during activities that typically do not bother the client, client's inability to speak. If any of these signs are present, the client may be suffering from exercise-induced angina, tachycardia, or asthma attack. Once exercise is ceased, if the symptoms do not go away, medical personnel should be called immediately. If the symptoms do go away, the client needs to seek medical attention prior to resuming exercise at the next session.

Common Metabolic Abnormalities

If a client is experiencing a metabolic abnormality during exercise, such as hypo- or hyperglycemia, the physiologist should be aware of signs that indicate it. Signs indicating metabolic abnormalities are as follows: fainting, syncope, pale face, blurred vision, dry mouth, excessive sweating. For clients with known metabolic abnormalities, it is recommended for them to bring something to eat or drink in case of emergency.

Open Wound

If a client has a wound that begins to bleed during an exercise session, the exercise physiologist should retrieve the first aid kit from the fitness facility. The client should be instructed to wash the wound with soap and water. The exercise physiologist should provide antiseptic and a band aid, and if necessary, help apply dressing. If the physiologist needs to apply dressing, she should wear safety gloves that are included in the first aid kit.

Complications with Musculoskeletal Injuries

If the pain does not interfere with the client's ability to express himself clearly, the exercise physiologist should ask the client what the pain feels like (i.e., sharp pain or dull pain); if the injury occurs in one of the limbs, the exercise physiologist needs to apply the RICE method where appropriate. If the injury is to the head, neck, or spine, the exercise physiologist needs to initiate emergency or first aid procedures depending on whether first aid staff are available at the fitness center. The physiologist should never attempt to move the client in this situation. Additionally, in order to remain within the accepted scope of practice, the exercise physiologist should ask the client to seek medical attention to treat the injury.

Complications of Cardiovascular or Pulmonary Issues

If complications arise during an exercise session that could indicate cardiovascular or pulmonary issues, the client needs to first lower the intensity of the exercise, assess heart rate to ensure it is coming down from where it was, and ask the client questions about how she is feeling to assess whether she can talk. If the client can't talk, the intensity of the exercise needs to be lowered further. If heart rate remains erratic, or complications continue, the client needs to initiate cooldown. After cooldown, the physiologist should stay with the client until heart rate is within 10 or fewer beats above the resting heart rate. Additionally, the client needs to drink some water.

Complications Due to Metabolic Syndromes

If complications due to metabolic syndrome arise during an exercise session, the exercise physiologist needs to follow protocol similar to when complications are due to cardiovascular or pulmonary issues. The exercise physiologist must keep in mind that the client should never be left alone during this time. If reducing intensity of the workout helps the client reduce symptoms of complications, the physiologist and client assess together that the client is able to continue the session, and no absolute contraindications are present, then the client can continue the session at the reduced intensity.

Ongoing Evaluation of Exercise Equipment

A fitness center should maintain its equipment according to manufacturer guidelines. Manufacturer handbooks should be kept on file and easily accessible. Machines should be cleaned between client use throughout the day, and clients should be encouraged and instructed on how to clean the machines as they finish with them. All equipment should be checked daily to ensure it is in working order.

Ensuring Safety Policies and Procedures Are Well-Known Among Clients

A fitness center should have all exits clearly marked. Procedures for emergency situations (fire, inclement weather, etc.) should be clearly posted. Additionally, the exercise physiologist should go through the procedures with clients to ensure understanding. Clients should be trained on equipment usage to avoid injury and to have confidence in using the fitness center on their own.

The exercise physiologist can assess client understanding of emergency procedures in a variety of ways. The physiologist can verbally go through the steps of emergency response with the client. Additionally, he can practice the procedures with the client and allow time for questions regarding them. Ongoing assessment should occur. The physiologist needs to be aware that it is his shared responsibility with the facility to ensure that the client understands all emergency procedures. The client should regularly practice all procedures.

If clients and staff don't properly understand how to act in an emergency situation, injuries can happen and unsafe behaviors can occur. Additionally, the fitness center can be held liable for any injuries or an unsafe situation that arises due to negligence. Procedures need to be put in place to safeguard the general well-being of the client/customer; if this is neglected, it becomes an issue of liability for the facility. If something were to happen to a client during an emergency that could have been avoided with proper training for the emergency situation, the fitness facility bears responsibility for that injury.

Necessary Steps of Emergency Action Plans

An emergency action plan for a fitness facility should consist of short, concise steps so clients and members can remember them. The emergency should be identified, a safe location should be designated in the proper area, and clients should be instructed on the proper path to that location. Emergency plans related to inclement weather (heavy thunderstorms or tornadoes) and fire should be in plain view and regularly practiced by facility staff and clients. Clients should be shown how to safely evacuate during a fire or seek appropriate shelter during a storm or tornado.

Spotting and Assisting During Exercise

Spotting and assisting clients with resistance activities allows the physiologist to ensure they are using correct form and not lifting weight that is too heavy for them to be using. This is an active way to teach clients while allowing them to learn in an active way. Spotting and assisting also ensures weights don't get dropped or roll away and others in the vicinity won't be injured.

Continuing Education

Continuing education is essential for the exercise physiologist to stay informed on the latest research and techniques in the field. It also allows for physiologists to get to know other professionals in the field. It keeps training techniques from becoming stagnant and ensures they are up-to-date and based on the most recent supporting research. Continuing education also allows exercise physiologists to specialize in a certain area and become aware of where their professional interests actually lie. Continuing education must come through approved providers to ensure that professionals are receiving the same level of education.

Keeping Up-to-Date with Current Research

Current research allows exercise physiologists to maintain understanding of changes in their field of practice and the scientific research that underlies those changes. This becomes important because physiologists need to understand the physiology of their practice and the reason for changes that need to occur. Understanding this information allows them to synthesize it and explain it to their clients in a way that makes sense, which ultimately helps maintain motivation and adherence to their exercise program because they understand why they are performing the specified activities.

ACSM's Code of Ethics

The ACSM code of ethics is a set of standards that govern all ACSM licenses. It includes guidelines on ethical practice, disciplinary issues, and exercise physiologists' responsibility to the profession and to the public they serve. Some examples of ethics related to exercise physiologists are the following: they must respect their clients at all times, they may not take credit for the work of other professionals in their field, and they must not claim the ability to perform services for which they are not certified. The ACSM code of ethics seeks to preserve a purity of conduct within all the professions it certifies.

Professionalism in Dress and Behavior

Exercise physiologists show professionalism in the way they dress by wearing professional attire that is not too short or too tight. Collared shirts are preferred, as well as proper footwear. The exercise physiologist should also maintain a professional manner with the client and other colleagues. Eye contact should be used during conversations, along with a pleasant facial expression. Where appropriate, refer to men as "sir" and women as "ma'am" unless the client indicates otherwise. When introductions are made, clients should be referred to as "Mr.," "Mrs.," or "Ms." unless instructed otherwise.

Ensuring Professional Activities Are Within Scope of Practice

The exercise physiologist should know the scope of practice and understand how to practice within its limits. Additionally, the physiologist should have a copy of the scope of practice within view so the clients see it as well. This sort of transparency ensures an optimal working relationship between the client and physiologist because the client knows exactly what to expect from the sessions.

Policies for Client Protocol

The exercise physiologist should know ahead of time the policies for billing clients, client cancellation policy, late arrival policy, and payment methods. For instance, if all sessions are payable up front, the physiologist needs to make this clear to the client. Similarly, the physiologist needs to let clients know how they may pay for their sessions. In addition, if tardiness or cancellation past a certain time is unacceptable and results in a charge for the session, the physiologist needs to let clients know this as well.

Mission Statement

A mission statement describes the vision, values, and expected service for a business. An example of a mission statement for an exercise physiologist would be the following: ______________ Exercise Services believes in empowering individuals to take control of their personal health and wellness. We empower our clients by teaching and modeling fitness concepts that develop strength and health for the entire body.

Negligence

Exercise physiologists can be tempted to practice outside of the scope of their certification, especially when clients ask for their advice on topics better suited to physical therapy or a rehabilitation specialist. It can also be tempting at the end of a long day for an exercise physiologist to become distracted and not pay attention to the client, which can increase the possibility of injury. Also, when the physiologist and client become very familiar with each other, they may be more likely to chat freely during the session. This sometimes encourages the exercise physiologist to not pay attention to technique as diligently as he might otherwise have.

Risk Management Techniques to Minimize Liability

Exercise physiologists must take care to keep their eyes and ears open at all times for the safety of their clients. Cell phones and anything else that would be distracting to the physiologist should be put away. Sessions should be properly documented so if any questions arise, they can be answered in a timely way. Where necessary, the physiologist should keep medical personnel up-to-date with pertinent information regarding the client. Clients should not be allowed to exercise on equipment that exceeds their current abilities, and physiologists should not promise to help with training details that lie outside their scope of practice.

Equipment Maintenance and Client Safety

Equipment should be checked weekly to ensure it remains in proper working order. If it isn't working properly, a sign should be put in clear view that puts the machine out of commission until maintenance is able to fix the issue. If equipment is broken, the client may be injured while trying to operate it.

Modeling Positive Behaviors

One of the most important things the physiologist can do for the client is to model positive behaviors. For instance, a courteous tone of voice when addressing the client, professional dress, actively listening to client issues, and not smoking are positive behaviors to demonstrate for the client. Additionally, it is best when the physiologist models the behaviors that he expects from his clients; for instance, being early to appointments, eating with proper nutrition, and exercising consistently during the week. The physiologist should have a "do as I do" attitude towards the client.

Manipulating Exercise Environment to Provide a Positive Experience

If the client is anxious about working out at a public fitness facility, the exercise physiologist can do a variety of things to ensure the client is comfortable. The physiologist should start with machines that the client is a little more familiar and comfortable with before introducing foreign ones. The physiologist should be early so she can greet the client, never making the client have to search for her to begin the session. If crowds make the client uncomfortable, the exercise physiologist can try to meet with the client during a time of day when the facility may be less crowded. The physiologist should make sure the client knows where everything is located inside the facility and ensure he has all the tools he needs to be able to exercise alone.

Limiting Distractions During Training Sessions

Exercise physiologists can limit distractions during a training session simply by putting their phone away and not having conversations with others who happen to pass by. Additionally, physiologists can limit conversation with clients during the session to what pertains to the exercise routine itself. Personal conversations can occur prior to or after the session. Clients should feel that all attention is on them for the duration of the session and that their money is going to a productive exercise session. Avoiding distractions makes the session safer and more enjoyable for the client.

Safeguarding Personal Intellectual Property

The exercise physiologist should copyright material that is his personal intellectual property. In order to do this, the physiologist needs to be familiar with national and international copyright laws and access the proper avenues to copyright material. Anything original to the exercise physiologist may be copyrighted and safeguarded in his name.

Documentation of Work Not Original to the Exercise Physiologist

Material that is not original to the exercise physiologist should be documented and cited whenever it is used. Physiologists need to be aware that even though information may be well known publicly, it must still be cited when used on blogs, websites, or printed materials. At a minimum, the title of the resource, name of the author, when the resource was published, and where it can be found should be included in the citation.

Developing Original Educational Materials

It is for the exercise physiologist's benefit to have educational materials ready for clients prior to actually needing them. When a physiologist first starts sessions with a client, she should ask the client what he would like to be educated on and perhaps give him a variety of topics to choose from. Materials should be formatted so they are concise and easy to understand. All educational material should be properly cited unless the information is unique to the exercise physiologist. Having personal, original educational material is valuable for a physiologist to have as part of her portfolio. Additionally, as the portfolio grows, it will benefit clients because there will be a wide array of educational topics for them to choose from.

Privacy and Confidentiality for Clients

The exercise physiologist can easily ensure privacy and confidentiality for a client by ensuring all computer files are password protected and information is shared only with those for whom the client has given permission. Information should optimally be shared over the phone or in person rather than email, or ideally, emails should be encrypted if they must be used. The rule of thumb is to make sure the client gives permission for passing on personal information.

Client privacy means that individual client information is privy only to the client it pertains to, and possibly to medical personnel. In some cases, the client may give permission for information to be shared with certain family members, but that permission should be obtained in writing from the client. Personal client information should never be shared over social media or with other physiologists.

FERPA and HIPAA Laws

The FERPA (Family Educational Rights and Privacy Act) and HIPAA (Health Insurance Portability and Accountability Act) laws protect the privacy of the individual. In the fitness profession, the exercise physiologist should only share what is minimally necessary for the benefit of the client and only where permission has been obtained. Client information should also be stored in a safe place that doesn't have public access, preferably under lock and key.

The exercise physiologist should follow FERPA and HIPAA guidelines where appropriate for his practice. Since health information is private and confidential, the physiologist needs to take every precaution to ensure it is not accidentally shared with inappropriate outside sources. The physiologist needs to make a practice of filing and locking client information and keeping it in his office rather than taking it to his place of residence.

Client Health and Contact Information

Prior to a training session, the exercise physiologist should always have the client's file where emergency contact information can be easily found. The physiologist should never begin a training session without having that client's file. The file can include session notes and previous workout sessions. This way, if the client has questions about her progress, the information is easily accessible in the moment.

Practice Test

1. Which are the two most commonly used arteries for checking heart rate by exercise professionals?

a. Femoral and carotid
b. Carotid and radial
c. Radial and femoral
d. Femoral and popliteal

2. If a submaximal exercise protocol is selected, what is the peak maximal heart rate that is allowed during testing?

a. 50 percent of predicated maximal heart rate
b. 60 percent of predicted maximal heart rate
c. 140 beats per minute
d. 120 beats per minute

3. Which of the following is NOT an instruction given to a patient during pretest instructions?

a. No food, alcohol, or caffeine should be consumed for 12 hours prior to exercise testing.
b. Wear clothes that are not tight to allow for free movement during the exercise test.
c. Ensure adequate hydration in the 24 hours prior to testing.
d. Get a good night's rest of at least 6-8 hours on the night before the testing.

4. What would NOT be considered a risk factor on a Health Risk Analysis when completing a health appraisal for graded exercise testing?

a. 46-year-old man hypertension
b. 52-year-old female with HDL cholesterol of 64 mg/dL
c. 60-year-old healthy male with a family history of heart disease
d. 35-year-old female who has unexplained fatigue

5. What is the most appropriate order for testing during a fitness assessment?

a. Resting measurements of heart rate and blood pressure, flexibility, cardiorespiratory fitness, muscular fitness, then body composition
b. Body composition, resting measurements of heart rate and blood pressure, cardiorespiratory fitness, muscular fitness, then flexibility
c. Body composition, resting measurements of heart rate and blood pressure, muscular fitness, cardiorespiratory fitness, then flexibility
d. Resting measurements of heart rate and blood pressure, body composition, cardiorespiratory fitness, muscular fitness, then flexibility

6. Measurement error in bioelectrical impedance analysis (BIA) can be due to all of the following EXCEPT:

a. Dehydration
b. Increased body temperature
c. Subject is placed in supine position during testing
d. Use of wrong predictive equation

7. What is the most appropriate reason for selecting maximal testing on an individual?

a. It is the most effective way to diagnose coronary artery disease.
b. It is the least expensive form of testing.
c. It does not require the presence of a physician.
d. It is the most appropriate way to test an obese individual.

8. What is the Cooper 12-minute test?

a. The participant must run a mile within 12 minutes.
b. The participant must go as far a distance as they are able to by running or walking within a 12-minute time frame.
c. The participant selects the form of exercise he or she is most capable of doing then must do this exercise for 12-minutes without stopping.
d. The participant has to use a treadmill for 12-minutes, and then vital signs are measured.

9. The use of thallium during an exercise stress test is useful for all of the following reasons EXCEPT:

a. Thallium can help to detect the amount of damage caused by a heart attack.
b. Thallium can help to determine a safe exercise prescription.
c. Thallium can determine ischemic areas around the heart up to 24 hours following injection.
d. Thallium can help ascertain the amount of blockage in any of the main arteries in the body.

10. You are asked to consult on a 42-year-old female for exercise testing. Her body mass index is 31 kg/m^2 and has fasting blood glucose of 122 mg/dL. The woman is also a smoker. She is not experiencing any symptoms of coronary artery disease. What would you recommend for clinical exercise testing?

a. The woman is moderate risk. She is asymptomatic and you recommend a medical exam prior to exercise testing followed by MD supervision of the exercise testing.
b. The woman is high risk and should receive a medical exam and graded exercise testing prior to clinical exercise testing.
c. The woman is moderate risk. She is asymptomatic and does not require a medical exam prior to exercise testing. She can undergo submaximal testing without physician supervision.
d. The woman is high risk. She is asymptomatic but should receive a medical exam prior to exercise testing due to risk factors. She can then undergo submaximal testing without physician supervision.

11. Which of the following best describes clinical exercise testing done before a patient is discharged from the hospital following a myocardial infarction?

a. Most insurances will only cover the clinical exercise testing if it is done as an in-patient.
b. It is necessary in order to determine what medications should be prescribed for the patient.
c. The most appropriate time for clinical exercise testing is at least three weeks following a myocardial infarction.
d. Clinical exercise testing is needed to assess the patient's ability to complete activities of daily life (ADLs).

12. Which of the following would be a relative contraindication to exercise testing?

a. Unstable angina
b. Poorly controlled diabetes mellitus
c. Acute pericarditis
d. Severe aortic stenosis

13. Low impact aerobics is characterized by which of the following?

a. Both feet may leave the floor at the same time.
b. One foot is on the floor at all times.
c. The use of steps of differing heights to achieve aerobic status.
d. Higher injury rates for individuals who are out of physical shape.

14. You are working to develop an exercise prescription with a patient who prefers low intensity exercise. Which of the following is FALSE about low intensity activity?

a. Low intensity but longer duration exercise is similar in benefits to high intensity exercise for shorter duration.
b. The risk for injury to bones and muscles are greater with higher intensity exercise.
c. The level of intensity does not matter as long as the patient reaches 55-90 percent of maximum heart rate.
d. High intensity is better and the patient should be encouraged to set this as a goal.

15. What would be the most appropriate statement regarding mode of exercise?

a. The more muscle groups that are engaged during exercise, the better the benefit.
b. A combination of three modes of exercise during a session is most effective.
c. It is more important to get a high intensity workout than to participate in a mode of exercise that is enjoyable.
d. Compliance to exercise regimen increases when walking is selected as the mode rather than running.

16. A pregnant woman in her twentieth week was referred to you by her physician for an exercise prescription. She is now 28 weeks into her pregnancy and has been diagnosed with incompetent cervix. Her pre-gravida body mass index was 32 kg/m^2 and she has a history of heavy smoking, but she did quit when she learned of her pregnancy. She has a history of hypertension, but it has been well controlled. Which of the following would be an absolute contraindication to continuing her exercise prescription?

a. Body mass index of 32 kg/m2
b. History of heavy smoking
c. Incompetent cervix
d. History of hypertension

17. Which would not be an appropriate alteration to an exercise prescription for an older adult?

a. Using a cycle ergometer for an older adult with balance issues.
b. Utilizing a handrail on the treadmill to help with support for an older adult with balance issues.
c. If a treadmill protocol is selected, the increase in the workload should be increasing speed rather than grade.
d. Altering exercise prescription to incorporate an intermittent protocol.

18. What would be an appropriate prescription for intensity level of exercise for a patient with cardiovascular disease (CVD)?

a. RPE of 8-10 on a scale of 6-20
b. RPE of 11-16 on a scale of 6-20
c. 30 percent of heart rate reserve
d. 85 percent of oxygen uptake reserve

19. Which of the following is not an example of advice that would be given for a patient with arthritis when developing an exercise prescription?

a. Increasing the duration of exercise is more beneficial than intensity
b. Emphasizing the importance of warming up and cooling down before and after exercise is essential
c. Shoes that help to absorb shocks are important and a visit to a specialized shoe store may be necessary to obtain appropriate footwear
d. It is important to schedule exercise at the same time per day and to work through pain in order to see benefits and improvement in arthritic symptoms

20. A patient with cancer has been referred to you for an exercise prescription. Which of the following would be an absolute contraindication to exercise for someone with cancer?

a. Platelets level of 42,000
b. Temperature of 99.8° F
c. Osteopenia
d. Moderate dyspnea

21. When planning an exercise program for an individual with diabetes mellitus, what is the threshold for blood glucose levels that should be identified pre- and post-exercise as requiring attention?

a. Less than 50 mg/dL
b. Less than 75 mg/dL
c. Less than 100 mg/dL
d. Less than 125 mg/dL

22. Which of the following best describes an exercise prescription for an individual with HIV/AIDS?

a. Aerobic activity 5 days per week, resistance training 2-3 days per week, maximum heart rate reserve of 50-70 percent
b. Aerobic activity 3-4 days per week, resistance training 2-3 days per week, maximum heart rate reserve of 40 to less than 60 percent
c. Aerobic activity 3-4 days per week, resistance training 3-4 days per week, maximum heart rate reserve of 30-50 percent
d. Aerobic activity 5-7 days per week, resistance training 3-5 days per week, maximum heart rate reserve of 40 to less than 60 percent

23. Which of the following is a true statement about cardiac output?

a. An elite athlete may have twice the cardiac output as an average person.
b. An athlete's cardiac output is greater mainly because they are able to decrease the stroke volume.
c. Cardiac output is lower in children than adults.
d. A normal cardiac output is 4-8 liters per minute.

24. Carl Lewis is a former Olympic sprinter who won a total of ten medals between 1984 and 1996. During his competitive years, what type of muscle fiber did his body mainly contain?

a. Type I
b. Type II
c. Type III
d. Type IV

25. The tiny sac-like clusters where oxygen and carbon dioxide are exchanged between the lungs and capillaries are called:

a. Pharynx
b. Bronchiole
c. Alveoli
d. Pulmonary arteriole

26. All of the following are true about the effects of maximal intensity exercise on minute ventilation EXCEPT:

a. Tidal volume is increased to approximately 10 liters
b. Minute ventilation is increased and breathing becomes deeper
c. Caloric expenditure increases
d. Respiratory rate increases to approximately four fold

27. What is the effect of maximal intensity exercise on cardiac output?

a. Cardiac output increases to 10 liters/minute
b. Cardiac output increases to 15 liters/minute
c. Cardiac output increases to 25 liters/minute
d. Cardiac output increases to 40 liters/minute

28. Which of the following would be considered moderate physical activity?

a. Walking at a pace of 2 mph
b. Walking at a pace of 2.5 mph
c. Walking at a pace of 3 mph
d. Walking at a pace of 4.5 mph

29. What is runner's anemia?

a. Anemia due to unexplained bleeding
b. Anemia due to iron deficiency
c. Anemia due to a lack of vitamin B12
d. Anemia due to expansion of blood volume with a concurrent decrease in hemoglobin and hematocrit due to foot strike hemolysis

30. At what altitude is one likely to start seeing an impact on physical performance?

a. 2000 feet
b. 3000 feet
c. 5000 feet
d. 8000 feet

31. At what approximate age does bone loss begin in men?

a. 60 years old
b. 50 years old
c. 40 years old
d. 30 years old

32. What information would you obtain from the pacemaker code DDDR?

a. Both the atrium and ventricle are paced and sensed, dual action can pace or hold pacing depending upon the chamber the event is located in, and the pulse generator rate is rate modulated through an activity sensor.
b. The ventricle is paced, the atrium is sensed in a dual chamber, and the rate is modulated.
c. The atrium is paced and sensed, the ventricle is sensed, dual action can pace or hold pacing depending upon the chamber the event is located in, and the pulse generator rate is rate modulated through an activity sensor.
d. Both chambers are paced and it is a dual chamber pacemaker.

33. In an emergency situation, all of the following are reasons that early defibrillation using an AED is important for sudden cardiac arrest EXCEPT:

a. Ventricular fibrillation is the most commonly witnessed event and can be effectively treated with defibrillation.
b. The chance of survival decreases very quickly without early defibrillation.
c. Within a matter of minutes, asystole can occur.
d. Any person who will operate an AED must be trained on the device prior to use.

34. What is the significance of a bruit noted in the femoral artery during a history and physical examination by a physician?

a. It is a normal sound that should be heard in all arteries.
b. It is indicates the presence of an aneurysm.
c. It may indicate stenosis or peripheral vascular disease.
d. It may indicate a deep vein thrombosis.

35. All of the following may help to medically manage coronary artery disease EXCEPT:

a. The use of Tylenol for prevention of blood clots
b. Prescription for nitroglycerin for angina
c. Lipid lowering medications used in conjunction with dietary changes
d. Weight loss

36. Which of the following is not a true statement about exercising in heat?

a. Any clothing should cover the least amount of skin surface area as possible and should be made of a lightweight material that breathes easily to allow for evaporation of sweat.
b. It is acceptable for a competitive athlete to lose 8 percent of body weight during competition.
c. Core body temperature will rise due to increased temperatures in the muscle groups as well as blood supply, and heat stroke may result if core body temperature rises above 104° F.
d. Heat stress can be prevented with acclimation. Those who are physically fit can tolerate heat stress better.

37. What is a general rule of thumb for fluid replacement to maintain adequate hydration?

a. Drink according to thirst
b. 3000 liters per day for an individual who performs at least an hour of vigorous physical activity every day
c. 10 mL per kg of body weight
d. 1 pint per pound of body weight measured before and after exercising

38. During exercise, what percentage of blood flow is directed to the skeletal muscles?

a. 55 percent
b. 65 percent
c. 75 percent
d. 85 percent

39. The primary risk factor for COPD is

a. Obesity
b. Pollution
c. Cigarette smoking
d. Pollen

40. Of the following choices, a person with congestive heart failure and systolic dysfunction would most likely have an ejection fraction of:

a. 35 percent
b. 50 percent
c. 60 percent
d. 75 percent

41. You are working with a patient in an outpatient cardiac rehab program and you observe the following symptoms: weakness on one side of the face, difficulty speaking, and confusion. You should immediately suspect which of the following?

a. Myocardial infarction
b. Stroke
c. Bell's Palsy
d. TIA

42. All of the following are true about the impact of cigarette smoking on health EXCEPT:

a. There is a 2.5 times risk for CAD in individuals who smoke.
b. Smoking lowers LD cholesterol levels.
c. The risk for developing CAD decreases by half within one year after an individual stops smoking.
d. A former smoker will have the same risk for developing CAD 15 years after quitting as that of a non-smoker.

43. What syndrome is associated with the following risk factors: hyperglycemia, hypertension, obesity, hypertriglyceridemia, and low HDL level?

a. Wolff-Parkinson-White Syndrome
b. Cardiocutaneous Syndrome
c. Congenital Heart Syndrome
d. Metabolic Syndrome

44. Which of the following psychological theories is based on stages such as precontemplation, contemplation, preparation, action, and maintenance?

a. Transtheoretical Model
b. Health Belief Model
c. Reinforcement Model
d. Relapse Prevention Model

45. When counseling a participant about beginning an exercise program, which of the following is the most effective tool to use?

a. Reviewing the health benefits of exercise using a slideshow presentation with the participant
b. The 5 A's (address, assess, advise, assist, arrange for follow up)
c. Using cognitive strategies such as reading books when in the later stages
d. Using behavioral strategies such as reminders in the earlier stages to establish good habits

46. What is the best option for dealing with a participant who has an overall negative attitude about life and complains often about the exercise program?

a. Ask the participant to change their attitude or leave the program.
b. Refer the participant to a counselor to help work on attitude.
c. If the participant is unwilling to change exercise habits, offer the option of leaving the program and arranging for a one on one program with an exercise physiologist.
d. Continue to try to work with the participant emphasizing health benefits and the importance of exercise.

47. What is the name of the federal organization that sets guidelines for safety in the workplace?

a. OSHA
b. FDA
c. HHS
d. CDC

48. All of the following would be appropriate initial treatment for someone experiencing heat exhaustion except:

a. Move the individual gently to a cool place.
b. Have the participant walk around until he feels better.
c. Use cool water on the participant's skin to help cool internal temperature.
d. If the participant is able, have her sip cool fluids.

49. Which of the following would be the main difference men would select a certain fitness center compared to women?

a. Availability of equipment
b. Price value equation
c. Location
d. Availability of programs geared towards kids

50. Which of the following would be a false statement about a pulmonary rehabilitation (PR) program?

a. PR programs are cost effective for patients with COPD.
b. PR programs can help to reduce length of hospital stays.
c. PR programs can help to improve respiratory symptoms.
d. PR programs improve the rate of survival in patients with COPD.

Answers and Explanations

1. B: Peripheral pulses are used to check resting heart rate by exercise professionals. The two most commonly used arteries are the carotid artery which is located on the side of the neck and the radial artery which is located on the lateral side of the wrist nearest the thumb. Other arteries that are less commonly used include the brachial (upper arm), popliteal (behind the knee), femoral (upper thigh), posterior tibial (behind calf) and dorsalis pedis (ankle). When a pulse point is ascertained, the index and third finger should be pressed gently over the site. The number of beats or pulsations should be counted in a certain period such as 30 seconds. The number of beats in 30 seconds should then be multiplied by two to determine the number of beats in one minute. Accuracy increases when the palpation time increases, therefore measuring the pulsations in 30 seconds are more accurate than measuring in 10 seconds.

2. D: Exercise protocols are selected based on a patient's past medical history, results of physical examination and the screening that was done prior to testing to identify risk factors already present. The exercise professional will select the most appropriate piece of equipment to use with the patient such as the treadmill or cycle ergometer. When selecting an exercise protocol for exercise testing, the next step selecting either submaximal or symptom limited types. Submaximal protocols have endpoints that are defined prior to starting. The most commonly used endpoints are 120 beats per minute or 70 percent of the predicted maximal heart rate. If a symptom limited protocol is chosen the patient will continue with testing until the patient experiences some sort of symptom or sign that indicates testing should stop.

3. A: There are certain instructions that should be given well in advance to patients before exercise testing occurs. The patient needs to get a good night's sleep of at least 6-8 hours to make sure he or she is well rested. The patient should make sure to drink enough fluids to maintain adequate hydration in the 24 hours before the test. Food, caffeine, and alcohol should not be consumed for 3 hours prior to testing. The patient should wear comfortable clothes that fit loosely in order to make exercise testing easier. The exercise professional should make sure the room temperature is between 68 and 72 degrees. The patient should be made to feel comfortable and at ease and the procedure should not be hurried along. The patient should also receive clear and concise explanations about what will be done and the purpose for it.

4. B: A health appraisal is a necessary step during the exercise testing procedures. It helps to identify those individuals who have certain risk factors that may need medical intervention prior to completing exercise testing. Risk factors include men age (men older than age 45 and women older than 55), symptoms of cardiac disease or previously established diagnosis of cardiac, cerebrovascular or peripheral vascular disease, certain metabolic diseases such as diabetes, and certain pulmonary disorders. Other risk factors may include a combination of hypertension, lipid levels, blood glucose levels, smoking, current fitness level, and body mass index.

5. D: If a person needs to complete the entire fitness testing in one session, there is a particular order that is recommended. The first test that should be done is any resting measurements that need to be take including heart rate and blood pressure. Next would be assessment of body composition. It is important that this be completed prior to any exercise portion because hydration status can affect certain types of body composition analysis. Next would be the cardiorespiratory fitness assessment. It is important to complete this testing before muscular fitness or flexibility because both of those can impact heart rate and not provide an accurate result. Next should come muscular fitness testing. It is important to allow appropriate rest time after cardiorespiratory fitness testing before tests are given for muscles. Lastly, flexibility assessment should be completed. At this time, the person's body has had time to warm up and stretch.

6. C: Bioelectrical impedance analysis (BIA) is a non-invasive way to measure body composition and does not require a highly trained specialist to administer the test. Two electrodes are placed each on the right hand and right foot. A small electrical current is used to determine the amount of fat-free mass, body fat, and total body water. Lean tissue is a good electrical conductor. Conversely, fat is not a good conductor thus interferes or impedes the flow of electrical current. Errors that may occur during testing are related to improper positioning of the electrodes, dehydration of the subject, incorrect body temperature, and using the wrong predictive equation for interpreting the results.

7. A: Maximal exercise testing is also known as graded exercise test (GXT) or stress test. This type of protocol uses small changes in physical workload and exercise requirements to push an individual to reach peak exertion or peak exhaustion. The main purpose of maximal testing is for diagnosis of coronary artery disease (CAD). This can be diagnosed even if the subject is not having symptoms. Maximal testing can also help to determine prognosis for someone who has a diagnosis of CAD and is also used to help determine an appropriate exercise prescription. This type of testing is typically the most expensive and requires highly trained clinicians to conduct the testing.

8. B: The Cooper 12-minute test is used in the field as a form of exercise testing. The individual or participant must try to run or walk as far as they are able to within a 12-minute time frame. At that point, the maximal oxygen consumption or peak oxygen uptake (VO_2 max) is estimated. Other field tests include the 1.5-mile test where the individual must run for 1.5 miles as fast as possible and the Rockport one-mile fitness test where the individual walks as fast as possible to cover one mile in distance. The heart rate is then measured 15 seconds after completion and the VO_2 max is estimated. Another field test is the 6-minute walk test where the individual walks as far as they are able to within a 6-minute time frame.

9. D: A thallium stress test is also known as myocardial perfusion imaging, nuclear stress test, or multi-gated acquisition (MUGA) scan. The reason thallium is injected is because it is a radioactive substance that allows pictures of the heart to be taken using a special camera. Thallium is injected and it enters myocardial cells based on how good the blood flow is in the myocardial cells. Thallium helps to determine blood flow when the heart is at its maximal stress level as well as when it is at rest. The amount of damage from a heart attack can be seen along with how much blockage is present in any of the coronary arteries. It does not check all the arteries in the body because there are other specialized tests used to look at other arteries such as the carotid or femoral. Thallium stress test can also help to formulate a safe exercise prescription for a patient.

10. C: Based on this woman's risk stratification assessment, she is considered moderate risk because she has greater than two risk factors for coronary artery disease. The risk factors she has are current cigarette smoker, a blood glucose level indicative of pre-diabetes, and weight. She dies not have symptoms of CAD which would include chest pain, dizziness, extreme but unexplained fatigue, difficulty breathing even at rest or with just a bit of exertion. Because she is asymptomatic, she does not require a medical exam or graded exercise testing prior to clinical exercise testing. For submaximal testing, she does not require physician supervision but if maximal testing is to be done, she would benefit from having physician supervision during testing because of her CAD risk factors. Maximal testing would push her to exertion and it is unknown how she would respond. Submaximal testing is not done to exertion. Instead the results are extrapolated based on the data obtained during testing.

11. D: It is important to complete clinical exercise testing prior to discharge for a patient who is recovering from a myocardial infarction (MI). The timing of the test before discharge helps to assess the patient's ability to perform ADL's on their own. It is also useful in determining functional status. The next time clinical exercise testing should be done is approximately 3-6 weeks following an MI. This time frame enables the clinician to assess progress since hospital discharge. It is also used to design the appropriate exercise prescription. Medications can also be adjusted based on results. Maximal testing is the best way to determine the severity of heart disease and can help to identify the amount of ischemia present. This in turn will help to formulate prognostic information.

12. B: When conducting exercise testing on an individual, many times there are risk factors present that need to be evaluated. Sometimes the risk of exercise testing is greater than the benefits that would be received and this is known as an absolute contraindication. Other times the risk of exercise testing is less than the benefits and this is known as relative contraindication. If the risk is determined to be relative, the decision can be made to continue testing with caution. Examples of relative contraindications would be poorly controlled diabetes mellitus, moderate valvular stenosis, hepatitis, HIV infection, hypertrophic cardiomyopathy, and ventricular aneurysm. Arterial blood pressure of greater than 300 mm Hg systolic or greater than 110 mm Hg diastolic is also considered a relative contraindication. Absolute contraindications would be any condition that would be potentially life threatening such as unstable angina, severe aortic stenosis, acute infection of the heart including pericarditis and myocarditis, uncontrolled heart failure, or recent myocardial infarction.

13. B: Aerobic activity is the type of physical activity that gets the heart and lungs working harder to provide increased oxygenation to the body. Low impact aerobics are geared more towards people who are not in the greatest of physical shape or for beginners. It has a lower rate of injury associated with it. Typically, only one foot leaves the floor at a time during low impact workout. High impact aerobics will have both feet leaving the floor during the session. There is significant calorie expenditure. There is a greater chance of injury with high impact aerobics. Step aerobics involves the use of steps to increase oxygenation. Overall, any aerobic activity is good. The goal for most people should be at least 30 minutes per day.

14. D: Exercise intensity is defined as the difficulty level of the exercise and how much exertion the body is pushed towards. Duration is defined as the length of time the exercise session lasts. Similar benefits are achieved with a low intensity but longer duration of a certain type of exercise as they are with a shorter duration but higher intensity exercise. In other words, you can burn as many calories with a short but fast run as you can with a more leisurely jog that lasts longer. The individual's preference should be taken into account on this. The fact that this patient prefers low intensity exercise should be the direction taken when planning the exercise prescription. High intensity exercise increases the risk for various injuries such as bone sprains or muscle tears. Other factors that should influence high versus low intensity is the age of patient, level of fitness, overall medical condition, presence of cardiac risk factors, and overall risk for injury.

15. A: Mode refers to the type of exercise one engages in. It doesn't matter what the mode is as long as the intensity and duration are such that good cardiovascular benefit results. When large muscle groups are engaged during exercise, the exercise is more effective. Riding a stationary bike is good but adding arms in with a different piece of equipment such as the elliptical machine or stair master is even better. During an exercise session one mode of exercise is acceptable; however, incorporating many different modes at various points can help increase interest and compliance. Using different modes of exercise also helps to cut down the risk of developing repetitive use injuries.

16. C: Exercise requirements during pregnancy are similar to that of the normal non-pregnant population, which is approximately 30 minutes per day most days per week of moderate intensity exercise. In pregnancy, it is recommended that the goal is at least three days per week. Those women who are obese or who did not have a very active lifestyle pre-pregnancy should always consult a physician before initiating an exercise program. In this woman's case, the incompetent cervix would be an absolute contraindication to exercise given the risk to the baby. Other absolute contraindications would be multiple gestation pregnancy with the risk of premature delivery, ruptured membranes, placenta previa after 26 weeks, persistent bleeding during the second or third trimester or restrictive lung disease. In these situations, exercise may compromise the integrity of the pregnancy and lead to death of the fetus.

17. C: Older adults who are in good shape and do not possess risk factors do not require a medical exam before initiating an exercise program. Many older adults, however, do have certain risk factors or issues that need to be addressed when developing an exercise prescription such as issues with balance, changes in gait or ability to do weight bearing activities. A cycle ergometer can be used as an alternative for those with balance issues, but the drawback is that leg muscle fatigue may set in more quickly. A handrail can be used on a treadmill to help with balance issue as well. If using a treadmill, typically the grade is increased instead of the speed to help offset any issues with gait. Intermittent protocols are also helpful where the exercise is divided up during the day. Another factor that may interfere with an exercise prescription is medication use which can impact heart rate and hemodynamic stability.

18. B: For individuals who carry a diagnosis of cardiovascular disease (CVD), it is imperative that certain precautions be taken when determining an exercise prescription. The overall clinical status of the patient, exercise capacity, threshold for chest pain/angina, and other risk factors associated with CVD. Frequency of exercise is similar to that of the average adult which is exercise on most days of the week. The intensity is prescribed based on a number of different methods. One common method is the rating of perceived exertion (RPE) scale, which is used to describe differing levels of exercise intensity ranging from no exertion to maximal exertion. The scale takes into account changes in heart rate, respiration, sweating, and fatigue. It is a subjective scale but has proven useful as an estimate of the actual heart rate during exercise. For patients with CVD, the RPE that is recommended is 11-16 on a scale of 6-20. This correlates with strenuous exercise, but the patient is able to continue.

19. D: Individuals with arthritis should strive to get aerobic exercise at least 3-5 days per week, resistance exercise 2-3 days per week and flexibility exercises should be done daily if possible. Functional exercise activities are also important to help manage activities of daily living (ADLs). The intensity of the exercise may difficult to increase related to pain but increases in duration are recommended alternatively. Individuals should try to time exercise based on peak activity of pain management plan and exercise should be avoided during periods of inflammation or arthritis flares. During this type of period, individuals should at least try to perform some gently range of motions activities through the various muscle groups. Warm up and cool down periods are essential for helping to deal with pain after exercise sessions. If the individual experiences increased pain after an exercise session for longer than two hours, adjustments should be made to the exercise prescription. Specialized footwear may be necessary to help maximize shock absorption.

20. A: Exercise testing for individuals with cancer is a gray area. The patient should be medically cleared for any exercise program prior to initiation. Exact guidelines have not been established but the recommendations have been written to reflect the general exercise guidelines set forth by the ACSM for adults as well as the American Cancer Society's guidelines of 30-60 minutes per day of moderate exercise at least five days per week. Special precautions must be taken in order to keep the individual safe. A platelet level less than 50,000 is an absolute contraindication to exercise because of the increased risk of bleeding. Other factors that may be present such as fever greater than 100 ° F, pain, fatigue, altered nutritional intake, dyspnea, osteopenia, as well as many others must be reviewed with the physician so a safe plan can be determined. High impact activities will most often need to be avoided because bone lesions or metastases are common with many types of cancer.

21. C: Individuals with diabetes mellitus are encouraged to obtain regular exercise as a way of helping to manage the disease. The benefits include better glucose tolerance, improved glucose control, improved insulin sensitivity, and potentially reduced requirements for diabetes medications such as oral hypoglycemic agents or insulin. Exercise also helps to reduce the risk for developing cardiovascular disease and helps with weight management. The potential for hypoglycemia is a risk for those taking insulin or oral hypoglycemic agents. Blood glucose levels should be measured before and after exercise. A blood glucose level less than 100 mg/dL merits attention. A carbohydrate containing snack of 20-30 grams is recommended. This is easily achieved with a serving of graham crackers or a serving of fruit. Timing of exercise is also important because of the risk of nocturnal hypoglycemia. Signs of hypoglycemia include sweating, shaking, confusion, and headache.

22. B: Exercise for individuals with HIV/AIDS may help to improve overall health status. Currently there are no specific contraindications to exercise with HIV/AIDS, however, the guidelines for the general population should be utilized. Aerobic activity should be done 3-4 days per week for a duration of 30-60 minutes per day and combined with resistance training 2-3 days per week. It is important to monitor exercise intensity to prevent a decrease in immune function with too intense exercise. This is measured by monitoring CD_4 counts. A general rule is to keep the heart rate reserve or maximum oxygen uptake reserve at 40 percent to less than 60 percent. An individual with HIV/AIDS who is healthy and asymptomatic may be able to safely increase intensity with supervision. Fatigue should not be a contraindication to exercise and may actually help. If the individual is experiencing nausea, vomiting, painful and swollen joints, exercise may need to be deferred until symptoms improve.

23. D: Cardiac output is defined as the volume of blood that is pumped throughout the body. This is typically measured in liters per minute. A normal cardiac output while at rest is 4-8 liters per minute. An elite athlete may have up to eight times the cardiac output as an average person. Stroke volume refers to the amount of blood that is pumped by the left ventricle during one contraction. Some blood is left in the ventricle. The heart of an elite or endurance athlete is very efficient at pumping blood and the athletes are able to increase stroke volume. Children typically have a higher cardiac output than adults do, but they oxygenate better than adults to compensate for this.

24. B: Muscle fibers can be divided into three types. Type I is slow twitch which are oxygen efficient and are able to produce more ATP for energy. Type I muscle fibers are used in athletes that are long duration and low intensity such as marathon running. Type II muscle fibers are considered fast twitch separated into IIA and IIB. Type IIA muscle fibers use a combination of aerobic and anaerobic metabolism to produce energy and IIB uses mainly anaerobic metabolism to produce energy required for quick and powerful activities such as sprinting. Type IIB muscle fibers have the greatest force, but get tired the quickest of all three types.

25. C: Air is inhaled through the nose or mouth and passes through the pharynx into the larynx. This process is called inhalation. Next the air enters the trachea. The trachea branches off into two bronchi which each lead to the lungs. The bronchi then divide into bronchioles. A capillary network provides blood to the alveoli which are located at the end of each bronchiole. It is within the alveoli that gas exchange takes place. The pulmonary arteriole carries oxygen-poor blood and the pulmonary venule carries the oxygen-rich blood. Exhalation is the process of expelling the carbon dioxide and other waste products through forcing the air back out of the nose or mouth.

26. A: Minute ventilation (V_E) is the volume of air that is inhaled and exhaled within a one-minute time frame. Resting V_E is usually around 6 liters/minute. This rate increases significantly during exercise with a concurrent increase in tidal volume. Tidal volume is the volume of air that is inhaled or exhaled from the lungs in a single breath. During maximal intensity exercise, the rate of breathing will increase as well as the depths of the breaths. This is due to the lungs trying to compensate for the increased work of breathing. The amount of calories required to support the increased workload increases which are one of the benefits of increasing exercise.

27. C: Cardiac output is the volume of blood that is pumped by each ventricle in a one-minute time frame. Stroke volume is how much blood is pumped from the ventricles in each contraction. Stroke volume is usually around 70 mL. Heart rate is the number of times the heart beats in a minute period. Cardiac output is directly related to stroke volume and heart rate. Normal cardiac output is typically 5 liters per minute at rest. During maximal intensity exercise, cardiac output can increase to approximately 25-30 liters per minute. This increase in cardiac output is necessary to support the increased work of breathing and delivery of oxygenated blood throughout the body.

28. C: The terms *exercise* and *physical activity* are often substituted for each other, but they technically have different meanings. Exercise is a form of planned physical activity that involves repetitions of certain body movements typically with the goal of enhanced physical fitness. Physical activity is movement of the body that involves the use of skeletal muscles and an increase in energy expenditure above resting.

Physical activity can encompass any type of activity such as walking, jogging, playing any type of sport, housework, or hard physical labor such as shoveling or digging. It can also encompass leisure type activities such as using a computer, fishing, playing an instrument, or light housework such as dishwashing. One way to compare various forms of physical activity is through the use of metabolic equivalents (METs). Light activity would be the equivalent of less than 3 METs, moderate between 3 and 6 METs, and vigorous greater than 6 METs. To qualify as a moderate activity, walking would need to be at a pace of 3 to 4 mph.

29. D: Runner's anemia is a condition often seen in long distance runners. It is due in part to an expansion of blood volume but where hemoglobin and hematocrit levels are actually decreased. It is unclear what the exact cause is may be related in part to the destruction of red blood cells while feet are pounding on the ground during running. Other possible causes are loss of iron in sweat or poor diet. In women, blood loss during menses may compound the problem. The implications of anemia in endurance athletes is that it will make the body work slower due to decreased oxygen availability and may affect performance. This can also affect energy levels and can cause muscle cramps and fatigue.

30. C: Low altitude refers to locations that are below 5000 feet, moderate altitude is between 5000 and 8000 feet and high altitude is between 8000 and 14000 feet. It is at 5000 feet that individuals will likely begin to feel the effects of being at a higher altitude and the ability to perform physically will be reduced. Acclimation to higher altitudes is recommended to prevent potential complications such as acute mountain sickness, high altitude pulmonary edema or just generalized difficulty breathing with frequent coughing spells. Acclimation is accomplished by staging an ascent to higher elevations. At least three days should be allowed for ascent to moderate elevation up to 5000 feet. An additional day per 1000 feet is recommended when ascending to higher elevations. It is also recommended that adequate hydration is maintained as well as frequent rest breaks. If any signs of illness are present, immediate descent to an altitude at least 1000 feet lower is advised.

31. B: Osteoporosis is a condition in which thinning of the bones occurs. This results in a reduction of bone mass and leads to weakened bones. The risk for fractures increases with osteoporosis and this risk increases with age. Men and women lose bone mass at different rates and different stages. Men start to lose bone mass at around age 50-55 years old. Women begin to lose bone mass much earlier at age 30-35 and this bone loss is greatly increased after menopause. Risk factors for osteoporosis include smoking, alcohol abuse, being Caucasian or Asian, family history, and lack of physical activity. Eighty percent of all individuals with osteoporosis are female. Inadequate calcium intake and vitamin D deficiency also contribute as well as certain medications.

32. A: Pacemakers are used to help normalize cardiac function and normalize cardiac rhythms. Common diagnoses that may require pacemaker placement are atrioventricular block or sick sinus syndrome. There are single chambered pacemakers that have one lead only in either the right atrium or right ventricle. There are dual chamber pacemakers that have one lead in the right atrium and one in the right ventricle. Pacemakers typically have four letter codes to identify its function. The first letter identifies which chamber is paced, the second tells which is sensed, the third letter refers to the pacemakers response to a sensed event (either no response, inhibits, triggers or does both). The fourth letter refers to whether the pacemaker is rate responsive or inhibited. A DDDR pacemaker is one where both the atrium and ventricle are both paced and sensed and the pacemaker can either inhibit or trigger depending upon the location of the event and it is rate modulated.

33. D: Automated external defibrillators (AED) are a type of computerized device designed to effectively and easily treat an individual without a pulse who is experiencing ventricular fibrillation (VF) or sudden cardiac arrest. The earliest an AED is used, the better the outcome. VF is the type of cardiac event that is most often witnessed and can be treated quickly with an AED. Without treatment, VF can quickly turn into asystole and death will occur. When faced with this situation, emergency medical services must be contacted, cardiopulmonary resuscitation (CPR) must be initiated, and the AED needs to be operated. EMS personnel can help guide a lay person through the appropriate procedure.

34. C: A bruit is defined as a rushing sound caused by the vibration in a vessel or artery wall due to rushing blood flow. This is not a normal sound and this is not normally heard unless there is a 50 percent occlusion in a blood vessel. As the vessel becomes narrower, the sound increases. A bruit in the femoral artery would most likely mean the presence of peripheral vascular disease (PVD). Common symptoms of PVD are pain and cramping in the legs or a tired feeling in the legs when walking or doing light physical activity. Risk factors include smoking, diabetes, hypertension, high cholesterol, obesity, family history, and lack of physical activity.

35. A: The medical management of coronary artery disease involves trying to keep symptoms under control and preventing the disease from progressing further. Medications are often prescribed for various reasons such as blood pressure control, angina management, and lipid lowering medications. Aspirin is often prescribed to help prevent clots from forming. Risk factors that can be modified should be addressed. This includes weight loss, dietary changes, blood pressure control, increasing physical activity, diabetes control, stress reduction, and smoking cessation. Cardiac rehabilitation is often recommended as a way for an individual to learn more about heart disease, how to address risk factors effectively, and how to initiate an exercise program.

36. B: Exercising in heat can be dangerous if proper precautions are not taken. Acclimation is recommended over a period of two weeks to allow for improved heat tolerance. Physical activity should be limited during extremely high temperatures and awareness of signs and symptoms of heat related disorders is crucial. Care must also be taken to properly hydrate. Competitive athletes may lose up to 5 percent of their body weight during competition, however, any weight loss greater than 1.5 percent should be identified and treated accordingly. Failure to replace lost fluids can result in serious medical complications. Possible side effects of heat stress include cramps or heat syncope which may involve fainting or near fainting. Another potential side effect of heat is heat exhaustion when there is excessive sweating, an increased pulse rate, hypotension, and/or difficulty walking. Heat stroke may also occur where there is disorientation, change in behavior, shivering and chills, loss of consciousness, and a core body temperature greater than 104° F.

37. C: An individual is considered dehydrated if there is a loss of greater than 2 percent of body weight measured before and after physical activity. Dehydration is dangerous and can lead to many complications such as increased core body temperature, change in mental status, increased heart rate, and other medical issues. It is important to be well hydrated before exercise begins. The risk of dehydration is greater for children who have not yet hit puberty, older adults, people who take diuretics and athletes who may intentionally try to dehydrate in order to make a certain weight before an event. Typically, 2000 mL per day is sufficient for most people to maintain hydration. A general rule of thumb for rehydrating is to measure pre- and post-exercise weight. Consume at least one pint of fluid for every pound of lost body weight.

38. D: The body has many acute responses to exercise. One of them is adaptation of the vascular system to better supply blood to the working muscles. At rest, skeletal muscles will normally receive approximately 20 percent of the blood supply. During acute exercise, blood 85-90 percent of the blood is diverted to the skeletal muscles and away from the liver, abdomen, kidneys, and skin. Other responses to acute exercise are an increase in heart rate, increase in stroke volume, and an increase in cardiac output. Systolic blood pressure will increase while diastolic blood pressure will remain the same or a slight decrease may be noted.

39. C: COPD stands for Chronic Obstructive Pulmonary Disease. This is a type of progressive lung disease that is caused by inflammation of the lungs due to some external cause. The primary risk factor for COPD is cigarette smoking although any inhaled foreign particles can also cause COPD such as air pollution or prolonged exposure to certain types of fumes. The symptoms of COPD include difficulty breathing due to shortness of breath, increased sputum production, and a chronic cough. It can encompass emphysema and chronic bronchitis. COPD is diagnosed through the use of pulmonary function tests (PFT). At the same time, a chest x ray will be taken as well as arterial blood gas to check how well the lungs are oxygenating and removing carbon dioxide. COPD is largely preventable. Damage to lungs is not reversible, but if the primary risk factor is eliminated, symptoms can be controlled and further damage can be minimized.

40. A: Congestive Heart Failure (CHF) is a form of heart disease where the ventricle is not able to eject the blood effectively for the ventricle or fill back up with blood. This can be due to either systolic or diastolic dysfunction. For those with systolic impairment, a low ejection fraction is commonly seen. This is sometimes due to coronary artery disease. A typical ejection fraction is somewhere between 45-70%.

This is the amount of blood that is pumped out of the ventricle during a contraction. With diastolic dysfunction, there would be impairment in ventricular filling. This may be due to cardiomyopathy. CHF is classified according to the level of severity ranging from Stage A, in which patients are at high risk for developing CHF, to Stage D, in which patients are at the end stage of the disease requiring a high degree of medical support such as ventilation or hospice.

41. B: The warning signs of a stroke are sudden weakness or numbness in one of the extremities, face, or one side of the body, confusion, difficulty speaking, problems with coordination, or a severe and sudden headache. The symptoms of a TIA or transient ischemic attack are similar, but they may go away after a short time. The only way to tell the difference is with emergency medical care. Emergency Medical Services must be contacted immediately because the sooner that treatment with a clot-busting drug such as TPA is started, the better the outcome will be. The risk factors for stroke are for age, family history, male gender, previous history of stroke, or TIA. Other risk factors include diabetes, hypertension, carotid artery disease, peripheral artery disease, smoking, a diet high in saturated fat, and lack of physical activity.

42. B: Cigarette smoking is a major independent risk factor for developing coronary artery disease (CAD). This is totally preventable mainly by not smoking and avoiding second hand smoke. Smoking can cause blood clots, increase blood pressure, and make exercise difficult due to interfering with breathing. Smoking also promotes a lowering of HDL levels, which are the protective type of cholesterol. Women who smoke and use oral contraceptives have an even greater risk for developing CAD. Smokers have a 2.5 times risk of developing CAD compared to non-smokers. Once smoking is stopped, the risk decreases by 50 percent after one year and after 15 years, the risk is similar to that of a non-smoker. Also, once an individual is no longer smoking, more oxygen is delivered to the heart.

43. D: Metabolic syndrome is composed of a group of risk factors that are metabolic in origin. If an individual has at least three of those risk factors, the syndrome is present. These factors include obesity, as defined by an increased waist circumference (greater than 40 inches in men and 35 inches in women); hypertension; glucose intolerance; elevated triglyceride levels; and low HDL levels. This syndrome is thought to be related in part to insulin resistance which can affect many systems in the body, including the kidney which helps not just to regulate blood pressure, but acts to increase triglyceride levels, and can increase the risk for heart disease in general. People most at risk for developing metabolic syndrome are age over 60, Asian or Hispanic race, and have a history of diabetes or pre-diabetes. Metabolic syndrome increases the risk for both diabetes and cardiovascular disease. The main treatment is weight loss, exercise, cessation of smoking, and increasing fiber in the diet.

44. A: The Transtheoretical Model (TTM) is also known as the stages of change model. The main belief is that individuals move through five different stages in their quest to achieve change. The stages are fluid, meaning that someone can go back and forth between stages. The first stage is precontemplation, in which the individual has no intention of changing current behavior whatever it may be. The second stage is contemplation, in which the individual is intending to make a change within six months. The third stage is preparation, in which the initial steps are taken to begin to change, but not at a consistent level. The fourth stage is action, in which the individual is making a concerted effort to implement the necessary steps to affect change. The last stage is maintenance, in which the individual has made the appropriate changes and has consistently made progress for at least six months.

45. B: Effective counseling techniques are so important in affecting change. During each session, it is a good idea to employ the five As: address the issues, assess the situation at hand, advise how to improve, assist with whatever problems might be encountered, and arrange for appropriate follow up. When trying to establish rapport with the participant, it is best to try to use an interactive method where the participant is asked questions, and the plan is appropriately negotiated to help encourage compliance. Other ways to build rapport include empathy, validation of the participant's concerns, providing positive reinforcement, letting the participant know you are there to help in any way possible, and to provide respect for the efforts being made. Cognitive strategies are useful in the beginning stages, such as reading appropriate books or watching a video to help encourage change. Behavioral strategies are more effective in later stages such as helping to find a buddy to partner with for exercise.

46. C: An individual who is a generally negative person and frequently complains is not likely to change behavior in a short amount of time. It is not recommended to discredit the individual's medical issues which may be helped by an exercise program; however, at some point it may be obvious that a change needs to be made due to lack of progress. The best option would be to stress the importance of changing exercise habits, but advise the participant that if he or she is unwilling to make adjustments, other arrangements can be made to help achieve the goals. One possibility would be working at home with an exercise physiologist in a one-on-one setting.

47. A: OSHA stands for the Occupational Safety and Health Administration and is a part of the United States Department of Labor. It was created through the Occupational Safety and Health Act of 1970 to ensure that working conditions are safe and will not cause harm or ill health. Some of the standards that are set forth that will help employees in a fitness center or healthcare environment are requiring the use of gloves, goggles, and any appropriate protective clothing when needed in dealing with participants. It is also recommended that good hand washing be practiced. Attention to safety is imperative such as keeping cords out of the way or keeping passageways clear. It also recommends that employees be well trained on any type of equipment they may be required to operate to prevent injury.

48. B: A participant with heat exhaustion will exhibit symptoms such as increased sweating, muscle spasms, tachycardia, feeling dizzy, possible fainting, hypotension, and slight increase in body temperature. Appropriate treatment would be to move the individual to a cooler area and remove as much clothing as possible. The individual should be lying down with feet elevated. Cool fluids can be given for the person to drink if able to. Cool water can also be used to on the skin to help reduce body temperature. In some cases, emergency medical services may need to be contacted or the person may need to be referred for immediate medical help.

49. A: Men and women choose a certain fitness center for a variety of reasons. Both men and women prefer a convenient location, convenient hours, a good value for the price, and staff that are of high quality as well as delivering excellent service. The main difference is that most men prefer a competitive center that has a good availability of equipment. Women, on the other hand, prefer a center that offers programs geared towards children. Women also prefer an environment that is non-threatening or intimidating and has the option of group exercise classes. The main reason for both men and women to join a fitness center is to get into shape and to maintain an exercise program. Another reason to join a fitness facility is the guarantee of a safe place to exercise with desired equipment available.

50. D: Pulmonary rehabilitation (PR) programs are an important facet of the health care system. Chronic obstructive pulmonary disease (COPD) is the fourth leading cause of death in the United States. There has been an increase in the number of deaths from COPD especially in females. PR programs do not improve the survival rate of COPD patients, but they do help to improve symptoms, reduce length of stays when in the hospital, and are generally cost effective. Some of the core components of a PR program are a physical functional assessment to check exercise tolerance, overall patient assessment to determine pre-existing medical conditions and history, education of proper breathing strategies, and the use of various types of respiratory equipment. Other core components are assessments on psychosocial factors such as quality of life a mental state. Counseling on activities of daily life, strengthening of respiratory muscles, and exercises to do at home are also components.

How to Overcome Test Anxiety

Just the thought of taking a test is enough to make most people a little nervous. A test is an important event that can have a long-term impact on your future, so it's important to take it seriously and it's natural to feel anxious about performing well. But just because anxiety is normal, that doesn't mean that it's helpful in test taking, or that you should simply accept it as part of your life. Anxiety can have a variety of effects. These effects can be mild, like making you feel slightly nervous, or severe, like blocking your ability to focus or remember even a simple detail.

If you experience test anxiety—whether severe or mild—it's important to know how to beat it. To discover this, first you need to understand what causes test anxiety.

Causes of Test Anxiety

While we often think of anxiety as an uncontrollable emotional state, it can actually be caused by simple, practical things. One of the most common causes of test anxiety is that a person does not feel adequately prepared for their test. This feeling can be the result of many different issues such as poor study habits or lack of organization, but the most common culprit is time management. Starting to study too late, failing to organize your study time to cover all of the material, or being distracted while you study will mean that you're not well prepared for the test. This may lead to cramming the night before, which will cause you to be physically and mentally exhausted for the test. Poor time management also contributes to feelings of stress, fear, and hopelessness as you realize you are not well prepared but don't know what to do about it.

Other times, test anxiety is not related to your preparation for the test but comes from unresolved fear. This may be a past failure on a test, or poor performance on tests in general. It may come from comparing yourself to others who seem to be performing better or from the stress of living up to expectations. Anxiety may be driven by fears of the future—how failure on this test would affect your educational and career goals. These fears are often completely irrational, but they can still negatively impact your test performance.

Elements of Test Anxiety

As mentioned earlier, test anxiety is considered to be an emotional state, but it has physical and mental components as well. Sometimes you may not even realize that you are suffering from test anxiety until you notice the physical symptoms. These can include trembling hands, rapid heartbeat, sweating, nausea, and tense muscles. Extreme anxiety may lead to fainting or vomiting. Obviously, any of these symptoms can have a negative impact on testing. It is important to recognize them as soon as they begin to occur so that you can address the problem before it damages your performance.

The mental components of test anxiety include trouble focusing and inability to remember learned information. During a test, your mind is on high alert, which can help you recall information and stay focused for an extended period of time. However, anxiety interferes with your mind's natural processes, causing you to blank out, even on the questions you know well. The strain of testing during anxiety makes it difficult to stay focused, especially on a test that may take several hours. Extreme anxiety can take a huge mental toll, making it difficult not only to recall test information but even to understand the test questions or pull your thoughts together.

Effects of Test Anxiety

Test anxiety is like a disease—if left untreated, it will get progressively worse. Anxiety leads to poor performance, and this reinforces the feelings of fear and failure, which in turn lead to poor performances on subsequent tests. It can grow from a mild nervousness to a crippling condition. If allowed to progress, test anxiety can have a big impact on your schooling, and consequently on your future.

Test anxiety can spread to other parts of your life. Anxiety on tests can become anxiety in any stressful situation, and blanking on a test can turn into panicking in a job situation. But fortunately, you don't have to let anxiety rule your testing and determine your grades. There are a number of relatively simple steps you can take to move past anxiety and function normally on a test and in the rest of life.

Physical Steps for Beating Test Anxiety

While test anxiety is a serious problem, the good news is that it can be overcome. It doesn't have to control your ability to think and remember information. While it may take time, you can begin taking steps today to beat anxiety.

Just as your first hint that you may be struggling with anxiety comes from the physical symptoms, the first step to treating it is also physical. Rest is crucial for having a clear, strong mind. If you are tired, it is much easier to give in to anxiety. But if you establish good sleep habits, your body and mind will be ready to perform optimally, without the strain of exhaustion. Additionally, sleeping well helps you to retain information better, so you're more likely to recall the answers when you see the test questions.

Getting good sleep means more than going to bed on time. It's important to allow your brain time to relax. Take study breaks from time to time so it doesn't get overworked, and don't study right before bed. Take time to rest your mind before trying to rest your body, or you may find it difficult to fall asleep.

Along with sleep, other aspects of physical health are important in preparing for a test. Good nutrition is vital for good brain function. Sugary foods and drinks may give a burst of energy but this burst is followed by a crash, both physically and emotionally. Instead, fuel your body with protein and vitamin-rich foods.

Also, drink plenty of water. Dehydration can lead to headaches and exhaustion, especially if your brain is already under stress from the rigors of the test. Particularly if your test is a long one, drink water during the breaks. And if possible, take an energy-boosting snack to eat between sections.

Along with sleep and diet, a third important part of physical health is exercise. Maintaining a steady workout schedule is helpful, but even taking 5-minute study breaks to walk can help get your blood pumping faster and clear your head. Exercise also releases endorphins, which contribute to a positive feeling and can help combat test anxiety.

When you nurture your physical health, you are also contributing to your mental health. If your body is healthy, your mind is much more likely to be healthy as well. So take time to rest, nourish your body with healthy food and water, and get moving as much as possible. Taking these physical steps will make you stronger and more able to take the mental steps necessary to overcome test anxiety.

Mental Steps for Beating Test Anxiety

Working on the mental side of test anxiety can be more challenging, but as with the physical side, there are clear steps you can take to overcome it. As mentioned earlier, test anxiety often stems from lack of preparation, so the obvious solution is to prepare for the test. Effective studying may be the most important weapon you have for beating test anxiety, but you can and should employ several other mental tools to combat fear.

First, boost your confidence by reminding yourself of past success—tests or projects that you aced. If you're putting as much effort into preparing for this test as you did for those, there's no reason you should expect to fail here. Work hard to prepare; then trust your preparation.

Second, surround yourself with encouraging people. It can be helpful to find a study group, but be sure that the people you're around will encourage a positive attitude. If you spend time with others who are anxious or cynical, this will only contribute to your own anxiety. Look for others who are motivated to study hard from a desire to succeed, not from a fear of failure.

Third, reward yourself. A test is physically and mentally tiring, even without anxiety, and it can be helpful to have something to look forward to. Plan an activity following the test, regardless of the outcome, such as going to a movie or getting ice cream.

When you are taking the test, if you find yourself beginning to feel anxious, remind yourself that you know the material. Visualize successfully completing the test. Then take a few deep, relaxing breaths and return to it. Work through the questions carefully but with confidence, knowing that you are capable of succeeding.

Developing a healthy mental approach to test taking will also aid in other areas of life. Test anxiety affects more than just the actual test—it can be damaging to your mental health and even contribute to depression. It's important to beat test anxiety before it becomes a problem for more than testing.

Study Strategy

Being prepared for the test is necessary to combat anxiety, but what does being prepared look like? You may study for hours on end and still not feel prepared. What you need is a strategy for test prep. The next few pages outline our recommended steps to help you plan out and conquer the challenge of preparation.

Step 1: Scope Out the Test

Learn everything you can about the format (multiple choice, essay, etc.) and what will be on the test. Gather any study materials, course outlines, or sample exams that may be available. Not only will this help you to prepare, but knowing what to expect can help to alleviate test anxiety.

Step 2: Map Out the Material

Look through the textbook or study guide and make note of how many chapters or sections it has. Then divide these over the time you have. For example, if a book has 15 chapters and you have five days to study, you need to cover three chapters each day. Even better, if you have the time, leave an extra day at the end for overall review after you have gone through the material in depth.

If time is limited, you may need to prioritize the material. Look through it and make note of which sections you think you already have a good grasp on, and which need review. While you are studying, skim quickly through the familiar sections and take more time on the challenging parts. Write out your plan so you don't get lost as you go. Having a written plan also helps you feel more in control of the study, so anxiety is less likely to arise from feeling overwhelmed at the amount to cover.

Step 3: Gather Your Tools

Decide what study method works best for you. Do you prefer to highlight in the book as you study and then go back over the highlighted portions? Or do you type out notes of the important information? Or is it helpful to make flashcards that you can carry with you? Assemble the pens, index cards, highlighters, post-it notes, and any other materials you may need so you won't be distracted by getting up to find things while you study.

If you're having a hard time retaining the information or organizing your notes, experiment with different methods. For example, try color-coding by subject with colored pens, highlighters, or post-it notes. If you learn better by hearing, try recording yourself reading your notes so you can listen while in the car, working out, or simply sitting at your desk. Ask a friend to quiz you from your flashcards, or try teaching someone the material to solidify it in your mind.

Step 4: Create Your Environment

It's important to avoid distractions while you study. This includes both the obvious distractions like visitors and the subtle distractions like an uncomfortable chair (or a too-comfortable couch that makes you want to fall asleep). Set up the best study environment possible: good lighting and a comfortable work area. If background music helps you focus, you may want to turn it on, but otherwise keep the room quiet. If you are using a computer to take notes, be sure you don't have any other windows open, especially applications like social media, games, or anything else that could distract you. Silence your phone and turn off notifications. Be sure to keep water close by so you stay hydrated while you study (but avoid unhealthy drinks and snacks).

Also, take into account the best time of day to study. Are you freshest first thing in the morning? Try to set aside some time then to work through the material. Is your mind clearer in the afternoon or evening? Schedule your study session then. Another method is to study at the same time of day that you will take the test, so that your brain gets used to working on the material at that time and will be ready to focus at test time.

Step 5: Study!

Once you have done all the study preparation, it's time to settle into the actual studying. Sit down, take a few moments to settle your mind so you can focus, and begin to follow your study plan. Don't give in to distractions or let yourself procrastinate. This is your time to prepare so you'll be ready to fearlessly approach the test. Make the most of the time and stay focused.

Of course, you don't want to burn out. If you study too long you may find that you're not retaining the information very well. Take regular study breaks. For example, taking five minutes out of every hour to walk briskly, breathing deeply and swinging your arms, can help your mind stay fresh.

As you get to the end of each chapter or section, it's a good idea to do a quick review. Remind yourself of what you learned and work on any difficult parts. When you feel that you've mastered the material, move on to the next part. At the end of your study session, briefly skim through your notes again.

But while review is helpful, cramming last minute is NOT. If at all possible, work ahead so that you won't need to fit all your study into the last day. Cramming overloads your brain with more information than it can process and retain, and your tired mind may struggle to recall even previously learned information when it is overwhelmed with last-minute study. Also, the urgent nature of cramming and the stress placed on your brain contribute to anxiety. You'll be more likely to go to the test feeling unprepared and having trouble thinking clearly.

So don't cram, and don't stay up late before the test, even just to review your notes at a leisurely pace. Your brain needs rest more than it needs to go over the information again. In fact, plan to finish your studies by noon or early afternoon the day before the test. Give your brain the rest of the day to relax or focus on other things, and get a good night's sleep. Then you will be fresh for the test and better able to recall what you've studied.

STEP 6: TAKE A PRACTICE TEST

Many courses offer sample tests, either online or in the study materials. This is an excellent resource to check whether you have mastered the material, as well as to prepare for the test format and environment.

Check the test format ahead of time: the number of questions, the type (multiple choice, free response, etc.), and the time limit. Then create a plan for working through them. For example, if you have 30 minutes to take a 60-question test, your limit is 30 seconds per question. Spend less time on the questions you know well so that you can take more time on the difficult ones.

If you have time to take several practice tests, take the first one open book, with no time limit. Work through the questions at your own pace and make sure you fully understand them. Gradually work up to taking a test under test conditions: sit at a desk with all study materials put away and set a timer. Pace yourself to make sure you finish the test with time to spare and go back to check your answers if you have time.

After each test, check your answers. On the questions you missed, be sure you understand why you missed them. Did you misread the question (tests can use tricky wording)? Did you forget the information? Or was it something you hadn't learned? Go back and study any shaky areas that the practice tests reveal.

Taking these tests not only helps with your grade, but also aids in combating test anxiety. If you're already used to the test conditions, you're less likely to worry about it, and working through tests until you're scoring well gives you a confidence boost. Go through the practice tests until you feel comfortable, and then you can go into the test knowing that you're ready for it.

Test Tips

On test day, you should be confident, knowing that you've prepared well and are ready to answer the questions. But aside from preparation, there are several test day strategies you can employ to maximize your performance.

First, as stated before, get a good night's sleep the night before the test (and for several nights before that, if possible). Go into the test with a fresh, alert mind rather than staying up late to study.

Try not to change too much about your normal routine on the day of the test. It's important to eat a nutritious breakfast, but if you normally don't eat breakfast at all, consider eating just a protein bar. If you're a coffee drinker, go ahead and have your normal coffee. Just make sure you time it so that the caffeine doesn't wear off right in the middle of your test. Avoid sugary beverages, and drink enough water to stay hydrated but not so much that you need a restroom break 10 minutes into the test. If your test isn't first thing in the morning, consider going for a walk or doing a light workout before the test to get your blood flowing.

Allow yourself enough time to get ready, and leave for the test with plenty of time to spare so you won't have the anxiety of scrambling to arrive in time. Another reason to be early is to select a good seat. It's helpful to sit away from doors and windows, which can be distracting. Find a good seat, get out your supplies, and settle your mind before the test begins.

When the test begins, start by going over the instructions carefully, even if you already know what to expect. Make sure you avoid any careless mistakes by following the directions.

Then begin working through the questions, pacing yourself as you've practiced. If you're not sure on an answer, don't spend too much time on it, and don't let it shake your confidence. Either skip it and come back later, or eliminate as many wrong answers as possible and guess among the remaining ones. Don't dwell on these questions as you continue—put them out of your mind and focus on what lies ahead.

Be sure to read all of the answer choices, even if you're sure the first one is the right answer. Sometimes you'll find a better one if you keep reading. But don't second-guess yourself if you do immediately know the answer. Your gut instinct is usually right. Don't let test anxiety rob you of the information you know.

If you have time at the end of the test (and if the test format allows), go back and review your answers. Be cautious about changing any, since your first instinct tends to be correct, but make sure you didn't misread any of the questions or accidentally mark the wrong answer choice. Look over any you skipped and make an educated guess.

At the end, leave the test feeling confident. You've done your best, so don't waste time worrying about your performance or wishing you could change anything. Instead, celebrate the successful completion of this test. And finally, use this test to learn how to deal with anxiety even better next time.

Review Video: Test Anxiety
Visit mometrix.com/academy and enter code: 100340

Important Qualification

Not all anxiety is created equal. If your test anxiety is causing major issues in your life beyond the classroom or testing center, or if you are experiencing troubling physical symptoms related to your anxiety, it may be a sign of a serious physiological or psychological condition. If this sounds like your situation, we strongly encourage you to seek professional help.

Online Resources

Due to our efforts to try to keep this book to a manageable length, we've created a link that will give you access to all of your online resources:

mometrix.com/resources719/acsmrcep

It's Your Moment, Let's Celebrate It!

Share your story @mometrixtestpreparation